THE
GIVEBACK
ECONOMY

Social Responsibility Practices
for Business and Nonprofit

Peter Miller and Carla Langhorst

Self-Counsel Press acknowledges the financial support of the Government of Canada for our publishing activities. Canada

Printed in Canada.

First edition: 2017

Library and Archives Canada Cataloguing in Publication

Miller, Peter (Peter Armour), 1942-, author

The giveback economy : social responsibility practices for business and nonprofit / Peter Miller and Carla Langhorst.

(Self-Counsel Press business series)

Issued in print and electronic formats.

ISBN 978-1-77040-294-2 (softcover).—ISBN 978-1-77040-486-1 (EPUB).—ISBN 978-1-77040-487-8 (Kindle)

1. Social responsibility of business. 2. Nonprofit organizations. I. Langhorst, Carla, author II. Title. III. Series: Self-Counsel business series

HD60.M55 2017   658.4'08   C2017-904975-5
                                          C2017-904976-3

Self-Counsel Press
(a division of)
International Self-Counsel Press Ltd.

Bellingham, WA   North Vancouver, BC
USA   Canada

CONTENTS

6 HOW THE ORGANIZATION WORKS

NOTICE TO READERS

Laws are constantly changing. Every effort is made to keep this publication as current as possible. However, the authors, the publisher, and the vendor of this book make no representations or warranties regarding the outcome or the use to which the information in this book is put and are not assuming any liability for any claims, losses, or damages arising out of the use of this book. The reader should not rely on the authors or the publisher of this book for any professional advice. Please be sure that you have the most recent edition.

DEDICATION

To all of the changemakers out there: The difference that you make is like an iceberg. The real impact that you make, you can't see as it is below the surface. It is how you get others to carry on your work that is the real changemaking.

CHAPTER 1
THE NEW ECONOMY IS HERE

The world is changing, for the better.

For thousands of years people have had to focus primarily on being self-serving for survival. What separates humans from other animals is the ability to choose the other's best interests over their own. We are able to resist our natural instincts.

Throughout the years, institutions have been created to help those in need. In the Middle Ages, faith organizations took on this role, with religious orders looking after everything from orphanages and hospitals, to feeding the poor. Along with faith organizations, in the late 1800s and early 1900s, large institutional charities emerged including The Salvation Army, The Red Cross, and The United Way. In many ways, the entire nonprofit sector emerged during that period.

Recently, though, this ethos has permeated society. The number of nonprofits that have incorporated in the last few decades has skyrocketed and continues to grow. This trend is expected to continue as the psychographics of people today has changed.

People want to make a difference. They want their lives to be meaningful. The new way to do this is to support a social cause.

Millennials are a huge part of this. *The New York Times* identified that millennials are more interested in making a difference, not just making money, and working for organizations that demonstrate community giveback strategies. Many are actively choosing employment within the nonprofit sector rather than a higher salary in the private sector ("More College Graduates Take Public Service Jobs," *The New York Times*, March 1, 2011). As millennials continue to emerge as the generation with the largest consumer dollars and take over the workforce, companies are seeing this as essential in terms of strategies in the giveback economy.

This is the emergence of true social justice rather than charity. People and organizations recognize the value and the relationship of giving versus what they get in return. Both sides are important for the giveback economy to work. Just giving or just receiving is not sustainable.

At the same time, we are seeing that the old paradigms of "profit, profit, profit" are no longer working. A giving back social responsibility strategy is becoming a necessity.

With the ethos of society changing, there is a trend that people don't want to just give their money when making a difference in the world, they want to be part of the change. A whole generation of youth wants to spend summers overseas helping to build schools in a developing country. People want to know more about how their donations are being used or are considering how to make an in-kind donation.

Volunteering is part of the high-school curriculum in many places. Beyond that, volunteering is considered an important thing to do during postsecondary education and even after graduation to improve one's résumé.

People are, however, not giving as much when it comes to money. Historically, giving 10 percent of one's income was a societal norm. It was ingrained in people to give during the weekly church service, or it was something that the neighbors would talk about. With the booming economy and the growing middle class during the 1900s, this was something that was achievable financially for the majority and it was driven through social pressures.

Today it is increasingly difficult for people to make the income necessary to live the middle class lifestyle, so there are and will continue to be a decreasing number of people who can afford to give 10 percent of their income to help others and an increasing number of people who need support.

Given the number of areas across North America which are not considered affordable, such as San Francisco, New York City, California, Vancouver, and Toronto, fewer people can afford to give money. The societal norms of giving are simply no longer normal.

Maybe part of the reason people are giving less money is that there are simply too many nonprofits using direct mail, and telemarketers that irritate consumers.

A social innovator with an idea can simply launch. There often might be a similar idea that is done in another part of the country, or even in a neighboring municipality, but there isn't a driving need to identify this in advance.

Why isn't the social innovator pausing to join or help expand an existing initiative? Most social innovators that launch an initiative are doing it for a personal reason, they are extremely passionate about it, and it is tied to their core values. They believe in it so much that they want to take personal ownership over it. When they do their research and see a gap in a single marketplace, it is natural to simply launch their own organization. They might see that other organizations are doing something about the cause, but it might be difficult to partner with an existing organization due to the work in getting buy-in or even the openness to work together. Rather than attempting to jump through hoops working with an existing organization, they launch.

Government social services no longer necessarily need to be run by a government organization or a nonprofit, and for-profits are entering the space and being awarded contracts to perform social services in a more cost-efficient manner.

For decades, for-profits have optimized their operations and minimized their costs, which has made them more cost effective (even when delivering a social service). Why would a government award a contract to an organization that costs more, is less value-focused, and without collecting taxes when compared to a highly efficient, value-adding, and taxable organization?

Garbage pick-up in many urban centers, a central service, has been outsourced to for-profit organizations that can perform the function at a fraction of the cost of the government itself.

In healthcare where there are nonprofits that provide the basics of care, there are for-profit organizations that provide supplementary services including blood tests or the logistics of managing medical supplies. In the United States, for-profit healthcare providers are often better managed and more efficient than their nonprofit counterparts.

As time goes by, more organizations are invited to provide social impact.

With all these changing paradigms, it becomes obvious that there is a need for something different. And along comes the emergence and increasing need for social innovation and social enterprise.

1. What Are Social Innovation and Social Enterprise?

The definitions of social innovation and social enterprise are still in flux as this important sector continues to emerge. In general, people are beginning to agree that the two are related, but they are only loosely associated.

Social innovation has a much wider scope than social enterprise. Almost anything that creates a social good that is a new idea can be considered social innovation. Meanwhile there are more specific definitions that are emerging for social enterprise, which we will discuss in a moment. Both are designed to make the world a better place.

1.1 What is social innovation?

With a wider scope than social enterprise, social innovation is all about ideas that make the world a better place by contributing to solving defined problems. Social enterprise can be a tool to create social innovation, but social innovation is possible without using a social enterprise model:

- This could be ideas for a nonprofit or charity. Example: An existing newcomer facility that starts providing legal support in immigration law.

- It could be ideas in a for-profit that will make a social impact. Example: The Beer Store in Ontario starting to recycle its bottles.

- It could be an individual or community group that decides to launch a project that makes a social impact. Example: A neighborhood garage sale that donates to a local charity.

It's great that the definition of social innovation is so wide that it allows more people and organizations to get involved to make a difference. The problem is that sometimes the scope is so large people and organizations don't know if it is actually a good fit for them. This may dissuade them from getting involved.

1.2 What is social enterprise?

Social enterprise has a narrow scope compared to social innovation with a lot of debate about what the final definition should be. Various organizations are defining this differently based on the personal outcomes they would like to see from the emergence of this type of organization, so the definition continues to evolve:

- **Social Enterprise Alliance (USA):** "A social enterprise is an organization or initiative that marries the social mission of a nonprofit or government program with the market-driven approach of a business."

- **Social Enterprise Council of Canada:** "A social enterprise is a nonprofit that provides a product or service to generate revenue for a further social impact."

Doing the right thing is becoming a strategy that is supporting the giveback economy. Might Starbucks through its fair trade program, or Walmart through its active involvement in fundraising, be identified as social causes and considered by some definitions as social innovation or social enterprise? Should it matter about the definition if an organization is doing the right thing?

In a recent survey by the Canadian Federation of Independent Business (CFIB), 99.3 percent of respondents indicated that they would like to give back to their communities in some way. People want to help each other and holistically want to make a difference in their world or community. They want to give back when they feel grateful for what they have.

One remarkable story is of a homeless person in Calgary who was struggling to save money after starting his first job in seven years. He was only able to bathe once a week, he didn't have a permanent residence, and the local church saved his money for him in a safe as he didn't have a bank account. When Fort McMurray's Red Cross fund was established, he was one of the first people to donate $40 from his savings. This is how 7 more than billion people can live on this earth together.

1.3 How are the definitions different internationally?

Social innovation and social enterprise are more advanced concepts in some parts of the world, with the United Kingdom leading the way in understanding and advancing this sector. Social Enterprise UK (socialenterprise.org.uk) states: "Social enterprises trade to tackle social problems, improve communities, people's life chances, or the environment. They make their money from selling goods and services in the open market, but they reinvest their profits back into the business or the local community." When they profit, society profits.

Social enterprises should —

- have a clear social and/or environmental mission set out in their governing documents,
- generate the majority of their income through trade,
- reinvest the majority of their profits,
- be autonomous of state,
- be majority controlled in the interests of the social mission, and
- be accountable and transparent.

International definitions don't tend to be the same and will mostly trend towards how the government has decided to prescribe its policies. Here is another example of how it is being defined, this time by South Africa's Bertha Centre for Social Innovation and Entrepreneurship:

"A good legal form for a social enterprise is generally one that allows it to combine multiple sources of capital, private and public, philanthropic and commercial, in order to advance and scale the impact of the enterprise. While South Africa does not have a dedicated legal structure for social enterprises, the current structures allow for significant flexibility."

1.4 Why is the definition of social enterprise important?

The various definitions and how they are applied now and in the future will have several impacts on social enterprises. Internationally, social enterprise is a movement that is happening so how the local governments handle it from place to place could be different.

1.4a Taxation

The definition will impact sales tax, income tax, property tax, and potentially other taxes by determining if social enterprises are exempt or if different tax levels will be created. For example, foundations are often required to have zero income each year (to balance the books to zero and not show a profit). Nonprofits are able to receive sales tax rebates. Churches are exempt from property taxes.

1.4b Granting

Granting by government organizations and related organizations will be impacted by the structure of an organization. Many types of organizations are not eligible for specific types of grants. As grants are extended to social enterprise, a more clear definition will be required.

1.4c Financing

Financing by organizations have a similar need to define social enterprises. World Vision seeks to create a social finance fund and would need to be clear on its investment strategies. Some credit unions are partnering with foundations to provide a blended grant and loan financing product that must be clear on eligibility requirements.

1.4d Government Request for Proposals (RFPs)

Requests for Proposals (RFPs) will increasingly be changing their eligibility requirements but may add in new ways for social enterprises to be included. This could involve a certification program or some other way to distinguish a social enterprise organization. One emerging example is Buy Social Canada or the Social Purchasing Project, that is qualifying social enterprise for municipal RFPs.

1.4e Government Policies

Government policies are always being adapted in order to encourage sectors that are deemed promising, critical, or in danger. With the emergence of social enterprise, future government policies are to be expected.

The definitions of social enterprise and social innovation have importance. However, at the end of the day, if everyone is trying to do good, this might not be worth arguing over.

CHAPTER 2
CORPORATE SOCIAL RESPONSIBILITY FOR EVERYONE

Are you making a difference? Is your life meaningful? These two questions are changing the world one community at a time and are bringing about the new economy: the giveback economy. People want to make a difference throughout their lives, in both their free time and in their daily activities.

Fernando is a marketing expert who is in his 40s. He has worked for many large, multinational organizations and is now in a director position. He doesn't like his job. In fact, outside of his work, he will openly discuss how he hopes to eventually move into the nonprofit sector so that he can make a bigger difference. But he needs to wait until he is senior enough so that he can still support his family on a nonprofit salary.

Mary is a retired middle manager who has been on multiple nonprofit boards since retirement. She volunteers more than 20 hours a week for various organizations and is always willing to lend an extra hand when needed. She won an award for her years of service and continues to believe in the importance of relationships. She takes part in programs that support the local community.

Chris is in his mid-20s and actively wants to make a difference not only in his volunteer hours, but during his working hours. Immediately upon graduation he traveled to Malawi to help the community. He has recently returned to North America and has sought jobs including working at farmers' markets and for a nonprofit.

No matter what stage of someone's life, the shift is on. The new economy is real and it is here. Companies need to embrace this and ensure that the work life of their employees makes a difference, or they risk losing these employees.

1. Corporate Social Responsibility (CSR)

Corporate Social Responsibility (CSR) is defined as the voluntary activities undertaken by an organization to operate in an economic, social, and environmentally sustainable manner. A socially responsible business model is perceived by customers and employees as doing right for the right reasons.

Corporate Social Responsibility = Social Investment. As soon as the term "investment" is used, it implies that there needs to be a way to measure the social benefits. Social investment means giving financially as well as in-kind expertise and volunteer in-kind support, as well as equipment and supplies. Through this effort there are measurable benefits to be gained as set out below.

CSR has taken many forms over the years on an ad hoc basis for some, and an organized strategy for others.

Initially it was perceived that just doing business and bringing jobs to a region or country was a good thing to do. Companies would be recognized as being good members of the community, especially when they employed a large percentage of the local population. This was quite common in car manufacturing towns such as Flint, Michigan, and those with other large industries including steel manufacturing, mining, and oil.

Bringing jobs to a community is no longer perceived as enough. Now, organizations need to prevent a negative impact as well. Walmart has been prevented from entering some markets to prevent local small businesses from being negatively impacted and thereby reducing local employment opportunities. Manufacturing plants have been dealt lawsuits due to negative health impacts to the local residents because of contamination of local resources from pollution.

 McDonald's attempted to enter the Jamaican marketplace. It launched stores and began to market. When the public realized that McDonald's wasn't purchasing local beef, they boycotted the restaurant. Eventually McDonald's left Jamaica, while other burger franchises have flourished by buying locally and supporting the Jamaican economy.

The recognition that organizations need to take responsibility for all of the positive and negative impacts they cause is increasing. Starbucks is concerned with recycling initiatives, ensuring that they are procuring fair trade coffee, and raising money for various charities to make further positive impacts. Many of these initiatives are reported on and considered strategically important. CSR initiatives are no longer a nice-to-have for organizations, they are a must-have.

Many organizations have recognized that donating employee time as team development exercises improves employee morale. This trend is continuing to grow. But with each hour that someone donates to a cause, they tend to feel that less financial contribution is necessary. An example would be if someone cut the lawn for a church, he or she might feel that he or she didn't have to contribute as much to the church financially as the person had saved the church thousands in lawn care. On the flip side, an organization without a volunteer strategy would miss out on these opportunities. This balance between cash and in-kind donations must be managed by the nonprofit or social enterprise as a CSR strategy is put into place.

CSR can and should be introduced in all sizes and types of organizations, including nonprofits and charities. They can all realize a number of benefits.

1.1 CSR for large businesses (multinational corporations)

Large businesses are implementing Corporate Social Responsibility (CSR) as a part of being in business. Just as it isn't a good idea to have no presence on social media, you also need to have a strategy for how you are going to give back.

This is becoming increasingly important as many millennials choose to work with organizations that make a social impact, even when they are offered lower salaries. Employee retention could be dependent upon CSR. In large businesses, CSR can be a department within or is part of a foundation set up by the company. It may also take a form within a retiree group or association where retirees volunteer with organizations and the corporation provides financial grants of support for a project or program.

There are plenty of examples of how this works today.

Virgin

Virgin has created Virgin Unite, which is a foundation that focuses on building the capacity of the sector. Over the last few years it has recognized that mentorship plays a pivotal role in the success of nonprofits, and it is actively investing millions of dollars in developing mentorship capacity around the world.

Walmart

CSR applies in Walmart as a department that connects with community and organizations to make a measurable difference in the lives of individuals and families. Two major campaigns include their annual fundraising drives with Red Cross and SickKids, where customers are asked at the register if they wish to donate to the cause.

Canadian Imperial Bank of Commerce (CIBC)

CSR applies in CIBC where retirees are involved in volunteer activities and can apply for financial support for the causes with which they are most engaged. This is a great example of how people don't only give money, but also give their time. In fact, people who donate their time become more invested in the cause and become more likely to donate financially as well.

CSR continues to evolve in a way to ensure that all parties involved are positively benefited. It is no longer as simple as a big company sponsoring a fundraising event. There are strategies for CSR engagement from the marketing department all the way through to the human resources department and it may take several forms.

1.1a CSR benefits for the large company

- Improve and increase brand name awareness locally, regionally, nationally, and even internationally.

- Recognition by communities and customers, employees, suppliers that the organization cares through actions, not just words.

- New sales, leads, suppliers, or referrals can come through these new interactions and positive image.

- Partnership introductions from the nonprofit or social enterprise to other businesses that support the same cause.

- Social media activity will increase when the large business is demonstrating its values through these relationships and this will be accessible to even more of the population.

- More press.

1.1b CSR benefits for the employee

- Executive and employee satisfaction in knowing that personal values are aligned with the organization. This can increase retention rates and even productivity levels at work.

- Employee networking and communication can be improved through many of these activities and events.

- Employee learning and skills development through volunteering activities. Typically within a professional context, employees may be limited within a specific role to mitigate the risk of the organization. But during volunteering roles that have a lower perceived risk to the reputation of the organization, the employee may be stretched in taking on new responsibilities and learning new skills that would be later applicable.

- Opportunities to provide employee recognition become available. Recognition is an important part of feedback and engagement for many people to feel motivated. This is another tool for managers to tap into.

- Community contribution will be made that will help with the overall local relationships and the work-life balance of the employees in the community.

- With the social good that is created, employees will have a sense of pride about where they work. They will tell people about their impact and the positive image of the large corporation. Endorsements (word of mouth) is the most trusted marketing (and you can't buy it!).

1.2 CSR for small and medium businesses

Corporate Social Responsibility (CSR) is not limited to only large businesses. Solopreneurs, micropreneurs, and small- and medium-sized businesses can also employ CSR as a strategy that makes a difference and provides benefits to the organization.

A solopreneur (a small business with only one employee) can apply CSR through a gift certificate, discounted pricing, in-kind support, or simply by sharing their skills, knowledge, and experience as a volunteer.

A Hairdresser

A hairdresser may be a solopreneur that serves local clientele by cutting hair in clients' homes. The solopreneur might become aware of a local drop-in center where marginalized individuals are unable to pay for a haircut, which further reduces their chances of positive social interaction or employment. The hairdresser may decide to volunteer once a month at the drop-in center and offer free haircuts to the clientele as a way of giving back or applying CSR.

A small- or medium-sized business can also employ a strategy to engage one or more community clubs, organizations, or nonprofits that change lives. Some provide support in terms of sports clubs and involvement in events. Some, however, do not have a clear strategy and plan that can yield significant measurable benefits, as discussed later.

A Restaurant Owner

A restaurant owner could provide a gift certificate for a dinner to a nonprofit that is running a fundraising event. The in-kind donation from the restaurant owner is only the cost of the food and service of the meal. However, the retail value of the meal could garner the nonprofit a large donation through raffling or a silent auction. The small business has now made an even larger social impact with its in-kind gift while improving its awareness in the community.

No matter how small, a business can make a difference.

1.2a CSR benefits to small- or medium-sized businesses

For the small- and medium-sized business, the impact of CSR will permeate the entire organization from the executives to the front-line staff. This includes but is not limited to the following:

- Giving back to the community and the improved perception of the organization locally.

- Direct recognition of contributions for programs and events that the business has done. This is a marketing opportunity for increased brand awareness and relationship building.

- Gain sales/leads/referrals prospects through the events and relationships built through volunteering.

- Gain partnership/affiliation introductions through the nonprofit and social enterprise relationships.

- Receive video or text testimonial for posting to website and social media.

1.2b CSR benefits for employees

- Executive and employee satisfaction and engagement in the business.

- Recognition for the employees at all levels both within and outside of the organization.

- Employee team building, learning, and on-the-job training.

- Networking with community organizations and people.

- Employees feel good for giving back and helping others.

A key part of optimizing these benefits is to ensure that the organization is identifying and measuring the benefits of applying a CSR strategy. For small- and medium-sized businesses this is more difficult to do with fewer resources, but it doesn't make the measurement and communication of any initiatives any less important.

2. How Does CSR Work in Business?

Large businesses are growing CSR as a necessity in their strategic and business planning activities, and many have assigned a senior officer to manage a department that plans and executes strategies.

They support community programs, events, and sustainability initiatives that make a difference locally, regionally, nationally, and internationally through many different and emerging methods.

2.1 Sponsorship

Sponsorship is when a business directly supports an organization, a foundation, an event, or even an athlete or person with a cash donation. Typically, sponsorships have mutual benefit for the large business as they are given awareness and marketing opportunities through their sponsorship. For example, if there is a sponsorship to a nonprofit, the sponsoring organization's logo might be displayed on a website in a prominent location thanking the organization for its sponsorship. At an event, the sponsoring organization might set up a banner or be given a display table to interact with the event's participants.

2.2 Fundraising

Fundraising in partnership with a large business can be extremely beneficial to a nonprofit organization or charity as they have a large number of stakeholders that they can interact with. Fundraising within the large business can be through —

- support for a program or an event such as entertainment, gala, speaker series, auction;
- a one-to-three day activity including a mailing from an executive to employees, or employees asking customers for a contribution; and
- selling a product or service for a fee.

2.3 Customer base

Especially with large, multinational organizations, being able to engage with the community and reach a large customer base can be hugely important. By partnering with a large business, there are many creative ways to fundraise directly.

One of the most common methods is the point-of-purchase ask which often occurs for direct-to-consumer offerings. The best known example of this is when checking out at a grocery store, the clerk might ask if you wish to donate an extra dollar to a charity. This has the benefit of high visibility as it is in plain sight, repeatability as the consumers would be asked every time they shop, and large volume due to the fact that everyone needs to eat and purchase groceries. Plus, the grocery store gets the visibility of doing this good deed in society.

However, the specific example of the grocery store is no longer as effective as it is overused. People don't like being put on the spot and the individual donor is not able to benefit from the tax break.

In the social sector, just like in for-profit, there is a need to constantly reinvent and be creative with CSR approaches so that they are successful. With any CSR approach, the key is to focus on the benefits for all of the people and organizations involved.

2.4 Employee base

Employees often wish to give personally, and working with large businesses opens up new opportunities to help their donations go further. Many companies offer matching programs, where the organization will match the donation of their employees. Sometimes these donations can be deducted from paychecks automatically so that it is easier for the employee to give more. Fundraising events can also add to engagement and communication within an office.

United Way

United Way works with corporations to host fundraising events in workplace settings. These range from pancake breakfasts to competitions between departments. At the same time they encourage annual pledges of giving from the employees, and the corporations are encouraged to match. In one instance, the corporation pledged to triple all donations of more than $1,000 per year, which helped the corporate employee campaign skyrocket.

2.5 Corporate foundations

Corporate foundations receive their start-up funding through the founders of the company or through a percentage of the annual profits. Often they have a specific mandate that is relevant to the corporation's values and is actively communicated internally. Sometimes customer-based fundraising also contributes to the total funds available for granting purposes.

Ronald McDonald Foundation

The Ronald McDonald Foundation contributes to children's programs nationally and is funded through point-of-sale donations as well as some of the profits of the company. These funds are allocated each year to charities and nonprofits across the country that provide direct support. This charity is part of the overall marketing of McDonald's Restaurants.

2.6 In-kind support

Monetary support is not the only requirement that nonprofits and charities need. In fact, often in-kind support is even more important. In-kind support can be pro bono or low-cost use of equipment, supplies, space, or other tangible items.

Alternatively, in-kind support can include pro bono services including marketing, strategy, or finance. Increasingly, large businesses are encouraging their staff to volunteer their time for events or programs. This has been shown to improve the perception of one's company as well as improving working relationships when the team or department volunteers together.

Habitat for Humanity

Habitat for Humanity builds affordable housing for families in need. It is able to do this by having the families and volunteers help in the construction of the homes, but also by saving on other construction costs including the building supplies. Relationships are built with building supply companies that allows it to get at-cost or donated products so that more homes can be built.

If Habitat for Humanity received donated funds to purchase the building products, it would be significantly more expensive than getting these at cost. The in-kind donation becomes just as important as a monetary donation in this scenario.

3. Social Investment

Social investment is a traditional investment in an organization in either a loan or ownership basis, with the intent in generating a small return while making a positive impact. This is increasingly becoming of interest as the traditional charity model of donations is harder to maintain. There is also an awareness that having an "investment" rather than a "donation" creates a different mindset in the nonprofit or charity. By thinking that this funding has to be leveraged to create financial sustainability, the nonprofit acts differently.

Although this type of funding isn't implementable for all nonprofits and social enterprises, it has increased the pool of money available to these organizations and has started the adoption of for-profit practices to be more embedded in creating social good.

Although there is no clear-cut answer to which types of contribution are the best from a large business, there are ways to partner between large multinational corporations and social enterprises.

4. How to Start CSR in Your Business

For all business sizes, a process can be used to employ a CSR approach and strategy to make a contribution to the community either locally, province/state-wide, nationally, or even internationally.

If your organization is new to this area, it is best to start with a core group of three or four employees supported by a senior manager as a sponsor. To help brainstorm how to get started, use the form called CSR Model — Policy, Processes, and Procedures available on the download kit included with this book. (See Sample 1 for an example.) With the help of the sponsor officer, prepare and present the form called Proposal Development to senior officers and obtain funding and resource support to execute (shown in Sample 4).

Start with small tasks and achieve small wins to demonstrate achievements. Next, propose a medium-sized project and engage more employees in the development and implementation steps.

4.1 Pick your CSR team

Determine an individual or small team with the interest and/or knowledge of CSR to lead the investigation of championing a CSR strategy. This champion or team would take ownership of both developing and applying the CSR strategy. It is important that any CSR strategy is actively supported by senior management and there needs to be continuous communication with the CSR team.

Note: Even starting up a CSR team will begin to see the benefits of engagement from the team members involved.

4.2 Gather resources

Ensure that the CSR team has a good foundation of information by conducting research. Find several examples of the policies, strategies, techniques, tools, and methodologies in planning and application to determine which work best for your business.

4.3 Understand the issues

Next, examine and evaluate a range of possible areas to consider for CSR. The most important part of CSR (and the reason you are considering this), is that you want to make an impactful difference. Make sure that the changes that you propose helping with or making are actually needed! Some possible areas include health care, environment, poverty, employment, support for people with mental and/or physical disabilities, cultural integration, immigrants and refugees, academic issues such as STEM, bullying, seniors' support, emergency preparedness and disaster management, or public safety.

4.4 Learn about the organizations

When considering applying a CSR strategy the next step is to research potential organizations (local, regional, national or international) that have similar core values and align with products and services offered by the business. (See Sample 2.) Part of understanding the organizations is often not just secondary research or information you can find online. It is beneficial for the team to go and meet with organizations to see what is happening at the grassroots level.

Sample 1
CSR Model — Policy, Processes, and Procedures

This form provides a basis for setting CSR policy, processes, and procedures, and should be included in your operations guide. It should be customized to the needs of your organization's policies and core values, drafted by the core team, and submitted to a senior manager/executive for review and approval.

What is included?

Marketing, team, operations, technology, finance

What is excluded?

Business plan, financial projections

Policy

Several policies will apply for each of the above areas and need to be dated and set out the authors

Processes

Best way to show processes is by way of flow charts with expected task times

Procedure

This area sets out what should be done to complete a task and can be used for training

4.5 Theory of change

Your theory of change is your strategic plan to make the long term change that you wish to see. This is called a theory, as it hasn't been proven until you have executed. So prior to success, it is considered a hypothesis. The change that you want to make here is usually a systemic change, which is a large change that focuses on the root problems and once implemented is unlikely to go back to status quo. A good example of a systemic change would be something as broad as poverty reduction.

Now that you understand the landscape, you need to determine how your business is going to make a difference. Often this starts with

Sample 2
Researching & Assessing Organizations to Work With

Use this form as a guide to determine what possible organizations to support through CSR. Start with a group and then narrow through analytics and rating based on specific criteria.

Fit Analysis

Geographic service coverage: [ ] Local   [X] State/Province   [ ] Country
                                    [ ] Countries

Core values similar? [X] Yes   [ ] No

Services align to company services/products?   [X] Yes [ ] No

Areas for CSR support (check all that apply):

[X] programs

[ ] services

[X] events

[X] social investment

[X] in-kind support

[X] employee volunteers

List of potential organizations:

Seniors Action Group

Conclusion and recommendations:

Connect at organization's office to see actions of staff

the change that you wish to make, and from that, working backward to determine the other contributing factors that could help make that change.

Consulting Firm

If you evaluated the subsectors and determined that poverty was a focus for your consulting firm, you would then realize that if more people had jobs in the area there would be less poverty. More people would have jobs in the area if there was better support for job skills training and more self-employment. Both of those could be supported through one-on-one coaching.

4.6 Choose how to get involved

Now you know that there is an issue. You have your theory of change to ensure that you will be making an impact. Now you can make a decision on how your organization will contribute, and your role in this space.

Depending on how you propose to support the subsector, different contributions would be more beneficial. The main ways to get involved can include financial, in-kind, and volunteering. (See Sample 3.)

Consulting Firm

Your consulting firm wishes to support poverty through one-on-one coaching support. As a consulting firm with coaches and consultants working for you, it is quickly recognized that the best contribution would be a focus on in-kind professional services or staff volunteering. This will have a much larger impact than cash donations based on the theory of change.

4.7 Communicate

To communicate effectively, start by developing a one-page proposal outline for communication to the president or executive director of the organization to connect to, outlining the proposed areas of involvement supporting services, programs, and events. (See Sample 4.)

Reach out to the existing nonprofit and social enterprise organizations that support this space. Look for idea partners and collaborative opportunities. Clearly identify the potential benefits to the charity/nonprofit/social enterprise and to the business. (See Sample 5.)

Where values and fit is aligned to have further discussions on how to collaborate, don't hesitate in setting up a meeting. It is always beneficial to be face to face where possible. Set out an informal agenda and plan for discussion. (See Sample 6.)

Once it has become obvious that this will be a positive working relationship, it is always best to get it written down between the business and the nonprofit or social enterprise. Document the agreement and then get a written contract or legal document.

Now it is time to put this plan into action. How can you move forward? What are the first small wins? (See Sample 7.)

Sample 3
Forms of Involvement

Businesses can review different forms of CSR involvement with one or more organizations on a one-time, monthly, annual, or several year basis. This can apply to an event, a league team, a program, or other forms of support.

A first decision is to determine the level of social investment in terms of financial, in-kind, and volunteer support that provides measureable benefits and a social return on investment.

Financial Support of $ __$5,000__ for __Seniors Action Group__ (organization)

In-kind resources (list all that apply)

Equipment
  Printer and server

Skills
  Website building and graphic design

Executive and Employee Volunteer Time
  45 hours

Estimated time and cost
  60 hours, $10,000

Sample 4
Proposal Development

This form sets out the one-page outline and one-page proposal and is developed by the core team to gain senior management approval for resources and funding to move forward. Additional information must be available to support sections of the document.

The document must be distributed to those who will be attending the presentation and will make the decision to proceed so that they are prepared to focus on the topic presented.

Use the following headings as a guide to prepare your proposal.

CSR Overview

Social innovation and examples

Social innovation can evolve in many areas such as health and wellness; housing and homelessness; crime and incarceration; and legal matters and can result in efforts to save lives, time, and money, and achieve positive outcomes that are measured.

In each of the above areas there are great examples of individuals who have created initiatives to address problems and create solutions.

Corporate social responsibility provides opportunity to give back to the community and brand the company as one that cares.

Our Organization's Proposed CSR Approach

What Are You About?

We formed a small core group of like minded people who wanted to find ways for the company to give back by working with one or more start-up or existing social enterprises, nonprofits or charities. We explored and researched several innovative and creative groups where we could help increase the impact on community.

What is the Problem and Who is Impacted?

We decided to find an organization that addressed youth homelessness, that impacted youth between 12-21, their families and friends, government, and the economy.

What is/are the Potential Solution(s) and Outcomes

Partner with 2 organizations that are nonprofits that need support to expand their programs and achieve measurable outcomes for the parties impacted.

Proposed Forms of Involvement

Social investment $ _$100,000_ for 1 year

In-kind support _skills to support workshops and mentoring and general volunteers_

Core team and other employees for a total of _125_ hours

Start and End Dates

Start _June 1_ End _May 31_

Measurable Benefits to Corporation and Employees

Sales leads and referrals from communities

Support brand name as a caring corporation to customers, employees, suppliers

Community recognition of company contributions

Employee satisfaction and pride in effort

Sample 4 — Continued

The following is a guide to prepare the proposal to be presented to senior management for approval.

Title Page

Executive Summary

Table of Contents

CSR Introduction

Organization to be Supported

    Vision

    Core Values

    Services alignment

Proposed Engagement

    Social Investment

    In-kind Support

    Volunteer Support

    Company Expense

    Duration

Benefits

    Company

    Employees

    Organization

Recommendation

Sample 5
Benefits

When investing money, resources, and time a business must be clear in determining what measurable benefits it should expect to gain.

The core team or project team must identify quantifiable and non-quantifiable benefits in the assessment stage and then prepare methodologies to clearly measure impacts when implementation is completed.

As outlined in the book some of the benefits can include the following and should include targets:

Sales leads/referrals	$1,500 plan	$1,875 actual
New partners/alliances	5 plan	12 actual
Indirect advertising and promotion	12 plan	22 actual
Employees developing new skills	25 plan	45 actual
Social media activity	1,000 plan	4,500 actual

Sample 6
Agenda & Discussion Plan

This form is a guide for preparing for the meeting(s) with organization(s) to determine if there is an exciting match that would be beneficial to both parties, and should be distributed prior to the meeting to parties attending. This may or may not include other stakeholders.

The agenda is a determinant of the structure of the meeting to ensure it is focused on by the participants and has potential actions going forward.

An example is set out below and may accompany a calendar invite so it could be logged in to each person's calendar with possible planning topics determined.

Date, time, location (could be a physical space or online using tools such as Skype or Adobe Connect) _____

Agenda

Welcome and Introductions

Participants – names and titles

Purpose _____

Organization Outline

Company Outline

Discussion of Proposal

Decision

Next Steps

Sample 7
Implementation Plan

This step outlines how tasks agreed to could be organized and assigned responsibility and start and end dates. Set out below is a simple approach which could be supported by a Gantt chart.

#	TASK	RESPONSIBILITY	START	END	COST
1	Complete project plan	Coordinator	June 1	June 15	0
2	Conduct orientation session with team outlining responsibilities and tasks	Coordinator	June 15	June 15	

A full-blown project plan could also be developed based on the complexity of the project(s).

Measuring is key. The results of the strategy need to be measured. Programs, projects, and events are only successful if they impact the parties involved. You need to be able to prove that this in fact happening.

Measuring happens at the end of the process, but measurement needs to be thought about on day one. Measure outcome results on those impacted including not only the nonprofit/social enterprise and its clients, but also the impact on the business, its employees, and its customers. For the company and the organization, include how outcomes measurement will be accomplished. This includes following up after the program or event to determine the value and the impact of the actions implemented with the parties involved. The results can be used by the organization to support continuation of the arrangement with the corporation and also used to apply for foundation or government grants.

It may take forms such as surveys, focus groups, or interviews that are documented and then analyzed, summarized with conclusions and recommendations.

Based on these results, you can determine how to adjust the strategy moving forward and hopefully make an even bigger impact to all those involved in the future. You also use these impact results to inform sponsors and apply for grants.

Being flexible and easy to work with are critical. With the landscape constantly changing, we can't be pigeonholed into what we assume will work and what we think the CSR program will look like. We often need to be happy with what people are willing to give when it comes to time and money. We need to be able to roll with the punches and adapt to what is available.

5. CSR in Nonprofit and Social Enterprises

For nonprofits, a process would help determine what level of support is needed, who to approach, how and what form of relationship should be established, and for what time period:

1. Define the problem and the solution. (See Sample 8.)

2. Research small and medium businesses that align with core values, products, and services that have similarities and synergies with the organization. (See Sample 2: Researching & Assessing Organizations to Work With.)

3. Define the "ask" in terms of financial social investment, in-kind support (expertise, equipment, products, referrals), and volunteer involvement (board of directors, board of advisors, committees, and event participation).

4. Develop a one-page document outlining the organization's purpose, possible alignment, the ask, and the benefits to the business. (Refer back to Sample 4.)

5. Direct or through referral contact the leadership of the business to explore a meeting possibility.

6. Prepare a five-minute sales presentation for the meeting to include how and why the business should become involved and what would be the benefits. (Refer back to Sample 5.)

7. Close the arrangement and formalize in a document outlining responsibilities and length of agreement.

8. Implement (Refer back to Sample 7.)

9. Measure results using outcomes measurement to show the impact of the involvement on organization employees, clients, and partners.

10. Evaluate whether to extend the arrangement.

Get started now: Find all of the forms that you need to set up your CSR strategy on the download kit included with this book.

5.1 CSR steps for social innovation and social enterprise

Many individuals and groups have ideas for unique projects that can contribute to changes locally, regionally, nationally, and internationally.

You must employ the following steps before implementing a full social enterprise approach:

1. Define a problem and determine the parties impacted.

2. Create a solution or solutions. (Refer back to Sample 8.)

3. Validate that the solution(s) meet the needs of those impacted, and that someone is willing to pay (some, or subsidized, or sponsor/donor/grant pays all).

Sample 8
Problem & Solution(s)

For both the organization and the corporation it must be clear what is being addressed for a product, service project, or program development.

This could include the following three-step process.

1. Define a problem and determine the parties impacted:

    Seniors would like to meet to learn and connect with different cultures in Chapel Hill, North Carolina. Seniors and their families are impacted.

2. Create a solution or solutions:

    Gain a government grant to use facilities and bring in presenters to discuss a variety of topics.

---

4. Research potential social enterprises, nonprofits, charities, corporations, academic institutions, governments, religious groups, and other organizations that you could partner with to develop and execute your solution concept.

As a social innovator or social enterprise you need to understand, apply, and employ CSR to help build your team and infrastructure in order to start and grow.

5.2 The key: Recognition and thanks

Having partners and working with businesses is great! It helps you make more of an impact through resources and through the extensive communication channels that are made available. The most important role of the nonprofit or social enterprise is ensuring that your CSR partners are recognized in every way possible. Many CSR campaigns plan for half of the budget to be dedicated to the awareness campaign.

Here are some ways for you to consider recognizing and thanking your CSR partners:

• Certificates (see sample on the download kit), pins, promotional items, T-shirts in recognition of executive and employee contributions

• Names and recognition on website, in programs, at events

- Press release, article, media interviews, and videos

- Video stories of receivers of support on website, social media, intranet, employee newsletter, organization newsletter, emails and text messages, LinkedIn

- Presentations to employees, clients, suppliers, community and business organizations by the supported group and their clients

- Awards, prizes, swag

- Testimonial: written and video (see samples on the download kit)

- Letter from executive to employees recognizing their contribution (for personnel file and portfolio and résumé) (see sample on the download kit)

- Letter from supporting organization (see sample on the download kit)

Social Innovation Challenge

The Social Innovation Challenge is a pitching competition for social ideas only that is building a network of social entrepreneurs and the collaborators that want to support them. When first starting up, it projected that it would need $200,000 in operation costs a year to run eight events. That was before it considered partnerships and CSR.

By reaching out to organizations while remaining flexible and easy to work with, the organization was able to bring the cash needed for annual operations to less than 25 percent of what had been originally projected. Venues were donated. In-kind prizing from large organizations was raised as opposed to cash prizing. The best part is that the winners of the challenge reported back that the in-kind prizing (including website development and strategic and accounting support) was more beneficial to its ideas than the cash would have been!

6. Relationship Benefits for Nonprofits, Charities, and Social Enterprise

It seems obvious that nonprofits and social enterprises will benefit from having a relationship with for-profit organizations that wish to be socially responsible, but there are some risks to avoid as well.

Benefits:

- Increase the amount of financial and in-kind donations.

- Gain introductions to other corporations/foundations/government offices through referrals.

- Gain new skills and competencies through skills transfer.

- Expand the pool of volunteers.

- Expand the number of influencers that you have in your network.

- Expand the number of people who can create awareness and help gain access to resources.

- Be affiliated with a successful organization.

- Learn from best practices from the for-profit organization.

Risks:

- The cause marketing could be superficial and not have the impact that you hoped.

- The partnering organization might have other causes or decide to cancel the campaign after a single year, leaving you without the forecasted financial resources.

- There are additional resources that you need to commit to this relationship including management time.

- The organization's activities or corporate values may not align with yours and blemish your organization's brand.

Prior to engaging in any relationship involving Corporate Social Responsibility, it is important to ensure that values are aligned, that both sides are willing to make the relationship strategic, and that you have ensured that it is a win-win relationship.

CHAPTER 3
YOUR SOCIAL IDEA

This chapter is all about finding that social idea and making sure it is a good idea.

1. Can Your Idea Change the World?

Social innovators are the heart of the social sector. They start by defining a problem, figuring out who the parties are, and how many people are impacted. Next they create their ideas, evaluate, and choose the best; a solution that solves the problem. Finally, they validate that the solution meets the needs of the parties impacted and determine who will pay for it (i.e., the customer), or the customer is subsidized, or the customer is fully sponsored.

Who comes up with social ideas?

- People who are working in a nonprofit, or charities who would like to introduce a new idea.

- People who are working in a for-profit who might want to create a foundation or nonprofit arm.

- People who want to address an existing cause and be an integral part of it.

Social ideas only happen when the idea is bigger than the innovator. It is important that you don't forget that you can't do this alone. In fact, the best social innovators are people who recognize that coming up with an idea is a small part of whether or not an idea works.

A study on what made social innovation projects successful by EDGE, a division of the United Church of Canada, indicated that the first things that any social initiative needs are the following:

1. Volunteers and the passion of the founders. Why is this important? It is an indication that there is sustainable leadership and it is also an indicator that the concept is compelling and that people would be interested in donating either their time or their money.

2. Partnerships and collaborations. Partners are so important that it was determined if you are working with more than 12 organizations, that is when the organizations become financially sustainable.

Although financial sustainability as a focus appears to be more of a for-profit or social enterprise goal, financial sustainability with a plan is required for all organizations including nonprofits and charities. If the long-term incomes of an organization are not planned for or known (no matter if these incomes are from donations or selling products), the entire organization is at risk.

It is with both the volunteers and partnerships that financial sustainability is realized. Long-term financial sustainability allows for longer term strategic planning and investment in the future, which inherently also increases the chance of a social initiative being successful.

Launching a social innovation is never easy. There are a lot of parallels between starting a for-profit business and a social business. Just like a for-profit start-up, there is a high chance of failure in launching and sustaining the organization.

In for-profit innovation, there is a general trend toward disruption of industries. Airbnb has disrupted the hotel industry. Uber has disrupted the taxi industry. It will be exciting for this trend to transcend the nonprofit world.

Warning: You might have the best idea in the world, but the best ideas have partners.

2. Where Do These Ideas Come From?

People come up with million-dollar ideas every single year. As people are becoming more and more socially aware and holistic, it becomes natural that social ideas will be more top of mind. So where do these ideas to do good come from?

2.1 Your life and personal experiences

Drawing from your life experiences is the easiest way to come up with an idea. It allows you to be passionate about it, have the knowledge to make it work, and you are a walking testimonial.

Your personal experience and what you have been through is the most common way to come up with a social idea. As the best social ideas are things that we are passionate about and care about, it makes sense that they would come from our personal experience. Personal experience includes anything that has deeply impacted us, from childhood memories to injustice that we have experienced to times of deep emotions.

Gordita's Closet

A young woman had always been plus-sized and had experienced both the emotional and physical implications of being overweight. With more than 50 percent of the North American population classified as overweight, this impacts millions. She wanted to create a thrift store for plus-sized individuals that would make them feel comfortable both emotionally and physically, with a ramp to the door, larger change rooms, and an area to relax and connect with others. She saw the gap in the marketplace she had experienced since childhood and wanted to support others like her.

Human Rights in Bangladesh

A young woman born in Bangladesh who moved to North America realized that she was privileged to have the higher standard afforded to her. With her personal experience of seeing a lack of human rights in Bangladesh, she felt that she needed to create an organization in order to advocate support for people in her home country.

2.2 Work experience

Your work experience could also influence an idea as you have been deeply involved in an industry or sector for a duration of time and feel strongly about continuing to support it. A lot of associations and advocacy groups are founded based on an identified need that the industry or sector has.

Centre for the Arts

A retired broadcaster who had done some writing as well recognized that there was no gathering place or performance venue for artists in a growing suburban town. He realized from his work experience that the power of an artist community was extremely supportive as well as necessary for the growth of the town. He started up a cooperative of artists and found a location for them to gather regularly and began the Centre of the Arts.

2.3 Your knowledge

Maybe the idea or the opportunity presents itself due to your educational background or from what you've learned throughout your professional experience. You could have a different perspective on an existing problem or maybe you can see where your skill set or knowledge could be repurposed for a social good.

Doctors Without Borders

The concept to have a group of qualified, socially focused doctors who were able to mobilize where and when they were needed specifically during disasters and in developing countries, capitalized on the many professionals who felt privileged and wanted to give back. Since the inception of Doctors Without Borders, there have been similar initiatives launched including Engineers Without Borders and MBAs Without Borders.

2.4 Hobbies

Your hobbies are things that you decide to do with your spare time. These are most likely activities that give you some sort of joy or self-fulfillment. This may inspire a social idea as you may hope that others would be able to feel the same positive way that you feel about a certain activity. Or you may hope that the activity may be more accessible for more people.

If you grew up playing basketball and it has been a very positive experience for you, then you might come up with the idea to teach youth basketball skills. Many NBA teams have launched basketball training programs for school children to inspire them to love the game and get the social benefits that the professional athletes might have realized as children.

2.5 New information

New information allows us to challenge our existing perceptions and think about what we understand in new ways. New information can come from many sources. This could include news, reports, documentaries, presentations, workshops, webinars, or any other items to which we are exposed.

2.6 New technology

Technology and how it is used is constantly evolving.

Techsoup

Techsoup is a nonprofit that is designed to help nonprofits within the technology space. They receive donated and low-cost software products from software companies and provide this to nonprofit organizations and charities at a low administration cost. This allows nonprofits to leverage technology without it being cost prohibitive.

Technology is impacting human resources with many jobs today that will no longer be required in the future, and many jobs of the future being things we haven't even thought of yet. Two decades ago there was no such thing as a social media coordinator! Jobs can also be virtual without the need for brick and mortar offices.

As technology continues to evolve, so will the opportunities within the social sector to take advantage of this. There are opportunities how to get awareness, how to canvas for donations, how to find clients, how to recruit volunteers, how to do bookkeeping, and the list goes on.

Mobile Giving

With the ongoing emergence of mobile technology and the shortening attention span of people, instant and on-the-spot giving is becoming increasingly important. Ways to give using a mobile phone is becoming something that is needed by every nonprofit. There are now online platforms that allow people to instantly give through their mobile phones and there are engagement platforms to help build a relationship with the donors. When there is a disaster someplace in the world, Red Cross is now able to set up instant alerts to their donors or network to have them text to a number to donate. This is a new way of thinking about giving.

2.7 New research

With science evolving and new studies being published daily, there are always new ways to help people. Sometimes the way to begin helping is direct, such as putting warnings on smoking packaging once studies were released that smoking was dangerous to a person's health.

A social innovator could develop new research in the area that he or she is passionate about. Simply gathering data is the beginning of data mining to find information that correlates. A social innovator might do surveys to find out what the impacted group is experiencing or needs. There could be focus groups or simply testing whether the new idea is a good one.

2.8 Feedback

Listening is critical. If you are an existing nonprofit, social enterprise, or charity, having a source of feedback is also a source of innovation. It is great to have testimonials, video stories, and case studies of what is going well, but true innovators always care about what could be improved.

Creative Church Outreach

A church was running an English as a Second Language (ESL) program that taught English to new immigrants in partnership with the local school board. The church had additional space and was hoping to serve another community need by working with local agencies. By listening to the students, they learned that access to legal support for immigration purposes was difficult. This feedback inspired them to launch a social enterprise that provided legal support for new immigrants.

2.9 New marketplace

Thinking about a new client base, geographic area, volunteer base, donor base, offering, or anything that is brand new for your organization is always a time of flux and innovation. Take advantage of this time that your mind is doing some nonlinear thinking and see what else you might come up with.

3D4MD

3D printers are something that have been used in many different ways including printing new, needed equipment and supplies onboard a flying spacecraft! 3D4MD considered how to use 3D printing for good within the healthcare sector. In remote areas, people do not have as much access to medical devices and in developing countries the cost of getting to these areas can be prohibitive. Leveraging 3D technology to print basic medical devices reduces the material cost, the distribution costs, and creates a social impact in a new marketplace.

2.10 Clash of life and new information

When you take your existing life experiences and couple them with new information, ideas will come like water from a fire hydrant!

Product design companies specifically go through brainstorming activities by exposing their ideation teams to new information. This continues to light sparks and help people look at things in different ways. One example of a brainstorming exercise is to put two generally unrelated products beside each other and to start thinking of ideas from just looking at these two items.

For example, a stuffed animal and an eraser beside each other could generate these ideas:

- A mini stuffed animal that could fit on top of a pencil.

- A stuffed animal whose nose is an eraser.

- An eraser that is in the shape of a teddy bear.

- A teddy bear pencil case.

You could do something similar in the social sector by matching an existing service with a new market. For example, if you looked at matching a food bank with teenagers and offering:

- Health and nutrition lessons with meal planning.

- Cooking lessons using the food groups.

- A potluck dinner where people make it at the location.

- Social activities before, during, or after a joint meal.

Another example could be matching an existing sector with a new type of technology. If you think about poverty and technology, what ideas could you come up with?

- An app that shows where services are available.

- A free technology center with secondhand phones for the homeless.

- An online platform that highlights where and how to give to the homeless.

Stone Soup Network

A minister was speaking with a family where the mother was going through cancer treatment and although they could afford the basics, they could not afford to go out for her birthday dinner. The minister approached a local restaurant owner who immediately offered a free dinner as he wanted to support people in the neighborhood who were in need. This evolved into an online platform that helps 12 ministers and social workers in the neighborhood match in-kind donations to families that are just above the poverty line, but are still in need.

3. Identifying the Problem: Social Issues and Concerns

There is no idea if there is no need. There needs to be an identifiable problem if we are going to try to solve it. This has been proven time and again in for-profit where a product or service is simply not marketable as people don't need it. The same is true for social impact.

3.1 Types of social challenges

Around the world there are different buckets of challenges that almost all communities struggle to balance in one way or another. In each community there is a slightly different focus based on where the biggest need is.

Before launching a social initiative it is important to understand that the social problem that you trying to address is something that is of concern for the community you are addressing this for.

The following are some social problem/cause areas that you might be interested in focusing on.

3.1a Economic impacts

Typically communities are interested in having a growing economy that provides jobs and a high quality of life for people. Anything that provides economic stimulus or job creation or investment in the area is typically seen as positive. Some of the major challenges that could directly be addressed by a social initiative might be the following:

- **Poverty reduction:** Where the most marginalized individuals in society are supported to have a higher standard of living. The measure of poverty is different by country based on the average wages or income and compared to the cost of living.

- **Employment:** Creating employment opportunities for marginalized individuals or improving the quality of jobs in the area. This could be for unemployed and underemployed people. Even support in starting self-employment opportunities would count.

- **Affordability:** Reducing the cost of living is the other way of improving the quality of life. If increasing the amount of wages or number of jobs isn't possible, is there a way to make transit, housing, food, and other basics more affordable?

- **Tax contribution:** Employment creates purchasing power and also taxes to support community services.

3.1b Social impacts

Typically communities are wanting to make social impacts in people's lives that are outside of the basics and allowing people to have a more fulfilling life. Often social impacts are specifically targeted to groups of the population or interests:

- **Children:** All activities that help to positively impact children from sports clubs to providing breakfast.

- **Seniors:** Extra support for seniors from social activities to transportation to engagement.

- **Health and wellness:** Any challenge that needs to be addressed from providing access to basic healthcare to engaging the population in being healthy and reducing obesity.

- **Arts:** Any support for artists or engaging people in art.

- **Integration:** Support of connecting people to each other of different age groups or cultures.

3.1c Ecological impacts

The environment and sustainability are of prime importance to everyone. These are social challenges that happen everywhere, are impacted by everyone, and have a lot of different opportunities for improvement:

- **Animals:** All ideas that protect wildlife or the treatment of animals.

- **Renewable energy and clean tech:** Any new solution that is doing things in a more sustainable way or leveraging technology to disrupt what we are currently doing.

- **Environment:** Any ways to preserve the environment and protect the earth, from recycling to conservation areas.

3.1d Holistic impacts

Relationships that people have with each other and the emotional well-being of us as individuals:

- **Relationship building and connections**: This is a new area that has been lifted up as important to help with cultural understanding, empathy, and the beginnings of collaborative opportunities.

- **Spirituality**: All initiatives that help people in their spiritual grounding or understanding of themselves.

These are not an exhaustive list of the social challenges that are out there. It is important to be clear that there is in fact a problem, and that that problem exists in the community prior to trying to solve anything.

3.2 How to know if it is really a problem

This seems simple: How do you know if you're really dealing with a problem? Quite often, social entrepreneurs make an assumption that if they are trying to make the world a better place, their idea must be needed. Why isn't this always true? It could be that the need that you are addressing —

- is just a symptom of a bigger problem,

- has another solution that has already been adopted that is as good as yours,

- has another solution that has already been adopted and the effort to change is too large,

- has a better solution that is being considered, or

- isn't as important as another need that the community has.

Fast Tip: Consider use of a mind mapping exercise to define all the elements of a problem in order to clearly define it. Also determine the level of priority and importance to the community members.

To make sure that you are spending your time on solving a problem that needs to be solved, there needs to be some validation. There are three methods that you can use to do this and often you want to do a combination of all three (as discussed in the next sections).

3.2a Root cause analysis

The first thing to analyze is whether you have identified the correct problem. Often, perceived problems are actually secondary problems to something bigger. Increasingly, foundations and the social sector have focused on the systemic change (the root problem or cause) rather than just the symptoms.

How do you do this?

Step 1: Start with what you believe the problem is and create a problem statement.

Step 2: Now ask "why?" Why is that problem happening? Is there another reason behind why this is happening? This should have created a new problem statement.

Step 3: Repeat these steps until you can no longer ask why. This usually takes at least three to five whys.

Example problem: African health concerns

Problem statement #1: People are less healthy in Africa.

Ask yourself why?

Problem statement #2: People in Africa have more health issues than elsewhere.

Ask yourself why?

Problem statement #3: People in Africa don't wash their hands.

Ask yourself why?

Problem statement #4: People don't have readily available access to water.

Ask yourself why?

Problem statement #5: People don't have a system or place in their homes that makes it easy to store water and wash their hands.

If you had tried to solve the first problem statement, your solution would look very different than if you are trying to solve the last problem statement. By getting to the root cause, you will have a better solution and be more confident that you have understood the problem. See Problems and Solutions in the Resources section of the download kit included with this book.

3.2b Secondary market research

Secondary market research is when you use existing information gathered by another source to validate your assumptions. This could be through statistics, white papers, surveys, and other information normally found in a library or online.

You can use secondary research to find the following:

- What the local priorities that the government or local foundations have highlighted as of importance.

- Organizations that are already in existence in your community and the type of support they are providing.

- Events and other resources that might provide more information.

- Trends that are happening internationally and how they could apply locally.

3.2c Primary market research

Primary research is when you have to go out and find the information yourself. This can be done through focus groups, interviews, surveys, observation, round tables (see Sample 9), and any way that you are gathering the information firsthand.

You can use primary research to find the following:

- If your target client is using something else for the need right now.

- If the community leaders are sponsoring another initiative or another challenge.

- How the target client could best use your idea and the impact it might have.

- If this problem is something that needs to be solved.

3.2d Do people care?

Social initiatives that are the most successful are the ones that are able to make people care about them. They should be compelling to the individual or team who want to donate their time and energy to the cause. If individuals care about a cause, this has a trickle effect to both

Sample 9
Round Table Agenda

Estimated time: 2 hours

Arrival:

- Offer something to eat ½ hour prior to the start
- Collect names and emails of participants if they want to be contacted
- Give out name tags

Part 1: Context (45-60 minutes):

- Why is this round table happening? (Facilitator)
- Elaborate on the communities and its strengths/opportunities (Politician/Guest Speaker)
- Mission and vision of the round table (Facilitator)
- Specific goal of the round table (Facilitator)
  - What are you hoping to achieve?
  - New ideas?
  - Finding effective partnerships?
  - Learning about the community's needs?
- The Need (Facilitator)
  - Why is the group deciding to do this?
  - Why this point in time?
- Where Are We Now?
  - Further background information of organization, if necessary
  - Different ideas that have emerged prior to the round table
  - Any limitation/constraints that need to be highlighted
  - Scope of the ideas to be under consideration

Questions (Facilitator)

Part 2: Brainstorming (45-60 minutes)

Group Breakouts

Break group into teams of 4-8 to discuss the questions posed (30 minutes)

Questions

- What are your responses to the congregation's vision?
- How can this church and this site serve the community?
- Is your group able and willing to share in this vision?

Group Presentations: Speaker for each group outlines ideas and what was discussed in the groups (20 minutes)

Open Dialogue

- What had resonance?
- Any specific next steps?

Thank you!

organizations and governments. Therefore a key to success is focusing on a problem that people will care about.

People care increasingly about a social challenge if the problem affects a lot of people, has a big impact, and if it impacts someone that they know or want to protect.

3.2e How big is the problem?

The bigger the problem, the more impact you are able to make with a solution. This is important information to share with people.

The easiest way to understand this is to identify how many people are impacted by the social challenge. Is this a local community, a state or province, an entire country, or a continent? Is it an age group? Or, explain what the worldwide impact is.

3.2f How does this impact people and who is impacted?

People care more about a problem if it has a hugely negative or positive impact on someone's life. The main problems might include hunger, loss, safety, etc.

Another impact is to demonstrate the positive impact that is missing and would be fulfilled. This could include art, self-actualization, happier emotions, or even improving the quality of life for those with an illness.

People care more about a problem if they know someone it impacts or who they wish to protect.

Can people see, or do you know, the people who are impacted? Often the social initiatives are successful because people interact with people that the social challenge impacts. Cancer is an example of this; everyone in North America has met someone who has been impacted by cancer themselves or through a loved one. This is in comparison to homelessness which is present in all neighborhoods, but where in some more affluent neighborhoods it is invisible.

Do you inherently wish to protect those it impacts? Children and animals are two groups that people rally to protect based on the fact that they cannot protect themselves.

4. Can You Solve This for the People to Whom It Matters?

Now that you have understood the problem and found the root problem that you need to be focused on, you must ensure that your solution is going to actually help!

Is your solution solving the problem? Is it solving enough of the problem? Creating your solution requires taking into account what all of the stakeholders are asking for. Especially when you consider the social sector, there are more people who need to be taken into account than if you were simply creating a for-profit business. Consider several solutions before taking the plunge and evaluate the time and cost to develop them and how much of an impact each solution would have on the group that it benefits. Sometimes the solution is actually a combination of several solutions.

How to brainstorm the different solutions? First, think, is there a better way to solve the problem? The charity model of an individual or person giving to another person or organization is a traditional lens of viewing social innovations. However, there are ways to make any solution to a social problem better. Consider thinking "inside" the box by simply improving something and making it more effective through resources, processes, procedures, or programs.

Systemic change is the where the solution is based on solving the root problem rather than all of the symptoms. The idea being that by solving the root problem, all of the secondary problems will eventually disappear. It should also mean that over the long term the problem does not revert to the original state as there is an ongoing impact that has been made.

Women and the Glass Ceiling

If the problem is that women are hitting the glass ceiling, a solution could be that women be given scholarships for leadership training. A systemic solution would be to create a policy that the board of directors needs to have a minimum percentage of females on the board.

Social justice is where the solution is based on everyone giving and everyone receiving. The concept is that no matter who you are or what station in life you hold, you need things and are able to give. It is this joint need that is part of making a social difference.

Soup Kitchen Dynamics

If the solution that was created was a soup kitchen, a charity model could be that the volunteers at the soup kitchen merely prepare the food and serve it. In a social justice model, both the volunteers and clients would be invited to prepare the food, and everyone would engage in conversation and eat together.

4.1 Clients

Clients are the people that the product or service that you are creating impacts directly. You are helping them with something. Sometimes this is not just the individuals, but the entire family. When you consider if your solution is solving the problem, you are addressing the need to consider the following:

- How will the clients find out about it? And how can they be confident that this will be helpful to them?

- How easy will it be for the clients to access this? Will they be able to access it?

- Are there any negative impacts that will be created by this solution? Could this harm them in any way?

- Are there other needs that this solution could also help to address?

4.2 Volunteers and staff

People are the engine behind any social initiative. You want them to be happy in their roles and feel supported as they have decided to be part of this. When you consider your solution, you need to consider the following for your staff and volunteers:

- What type of roles are needed?

- Is this something that will be rewarding with a clear outline of the benefits that the volunteers or staff might receive? Could they network, gain new skills or experience, could this improve their résumés, or is there recognition?

- Does this require a high number of volunteers/staff? Do they have regular hours or could they be flexible or both?

- How will you recruit, retain, and recognize people? Will this be a sustainable program?

4.3 Donors and foundations

Funders are a critical stakeholder to consider when creating your solution:

- Is the solution making enough of an impact?

- Is there a clear list of benefits for the donors or funders?

- Are you able to measure the impact and demonstrate this to them?

- Are you able to come up with other forms of income beyond donations and grants?

4.4 Community partners and other stakeholders

Depending on your social initiative, there could be a multitude of stakeholders that need to be considered. Here are some other questions to think about in relation to your solution:

- How can partners and other stakeholders be included?

- Is there a clear list of benefits for the community partners and other stakeholders?

- How do you ensure that there is communication and ongoing engagement with community partners and other stakeholders?

- Are there ways to solve more of the problem by working with other stakeholders?

By considering all of the stakeholders and working with them to create your social initiative, you are much more likely to be successful and make the impact that you hope to make.

5. Proof of Concept

Before launching your social initiative, you need to prove your idea will work. You need to validate the idea. The best way to do this is to prove that you are not alone and that others support your solution. Here are some ways to go about doing this. (See Sample 10.)

Sample 10
Proof of Concept

Get Volunteers

Getting volunteers is a great way to prove your concept. In fact, most nonprofit ideas rely on a strong volunteer base. Examples:

- If you are creating a café, you would want to have people make specific time commitments to volunteer.
- If you are starting up an open mic in a community center, you would want to have volunteers signed up to bake cookies and make coffee for the first three months.

Get Partners

Having other organizations wanting to be part of your project proves that your idea will fly. Examples:

1. If you are starting a new youth initiative, and a local youth organization wants to help you market it.
2. If you are creating an event, and another organization wants to support it.

Get Donors

If someone is willing to give money to support your idea, that is proof that your idea is viable. Examples:

- If you are doing a fundraising event, and another organization sponsors it.
- If you are putting on a musical theater production, and someone donates toward a much needed audio system.

Get Investors

The more organizations and people supporting your idea, the better. If you already have one organization investing in your idea, it is a good sign that it is viable. Examples:

- If you are doing a new initiative that is supported by the another organization or another fund.
- If you are doing a community outreach project that is sponsored by another foundation.

Get Clients

The best way to prove your concept is to actually show that a product or service is marketable and that the idea works. Examples:

- If your idea is that you wish to sell homemade apple pies, you would want an agreement in place with someone to distribute your apple pies.
- If you want to prove that yoga church works, you should pilot it for at least a month and see how many people attend.

5.1 Get volunteers

Getting volunteers is the best way to prove that your social initiative will work. To get a social initiative off the ground, the first action is a group of passionate and dedicated volunteers that believe in the idea. Having a list of volunteers who wish to be engaged, or better yet are already helping, is a good way to prove your concept.

Free Legal Services for New Immigrants

An English as a Second Language school heard that their students needed help in getting immigrant legal support. They spoke to a local immigration lawyer who volunteered to come in once a month and support the initiative. The lawyer gained many benefits including name recognition, a way to give back, client leads and referrals, and recognition of contributions to the community.

5.2 Get partners

If other organizations want to collaborate with you and be part of your social initiative, it is probably a good idea! You can have partners sign up to promote it; volunteer at it; integrate it as a new product or service; incorporate it into a program or event; manage it through an intrapreneur; be a donor or sponsor; or provide in-kind support in terms of supplies, equipment, and skills.

Center for the Arts

A community center wished to promote arts in a medium-sized town which didn't have an arts presence. They created a roundtable to see if arts organizations in the region would want to take part and were pleasantly surprised to have 12 show up and agree to work collectively.

5.3 Get donors or investors

Having someone commit funding to your social idea as either a donor or social investor or funder is a great indication that you have a good idea. It is advisable to have a package for social investment opportunities that highlights the benefits to the investors and also how and when reporting will be provided.

Social Mentor Network

A network was being proposed to match social initiatives with business mentors to help ideas get off the ground. It was determined that this would need some infrastructure and start-up funding to test. During the ideation stage, two foundations agreed to co-fund the launch months before the idea was ready to launch.

5.4 Get clients

The best way to know if your idea is worth it is to get clients. Clients don't always just have to pay to prove the idea is good. Clients could pay, but could also be subsidized or fully sponsored. You need to prove that clients actually want your product or service and that it has an impact. Once you prove this, you can proceed to execute the idea.

Indigenous Cross Training

An indigenous resource center was considering new ways to support its community. They heard that elders wanted to learn to use technology. They heard the youth were interested in their elders' stories. By blending these needs into a technology course that would share the elders' stories online, they were able to create a new cross-training program where the youth heard the stories while teaching the elders how to use technology. Immediately they had registrations, and were able to launch the program within two months, with early registrations confirming interest.

Fast Tip: Could you partner? Does this need to be an independent organization? A large proportion of independent business owners start their own businesses in part for notoriety. With the ethos of social innovation, this is less likely. But it is a common trap to fall into. As you are thinking about starting your idea, you must be clear about why you want to start it.

Could this make more impact if you decided to partner the idea with an organization that is already in existence? The counterargument of doing this independently is strongly reinforced throughout this book as ideas in existing organizations and with partnerships are far more likely to make the intended impact.

CHAPTER 4
MARKETING YOUR SOCIAL INITIATIVE

Overcommunication is the name of the game when it comes to marketing.

For-profit companies get this. They understand that if you aren't making sales, you won't have a business for much longer. They come up with elaborate marketing strategies and spend copious amounts of time and dollars in figuring out how to do this well.

The nonprofit and social enterprise world has always had a very different culture. It is a culture of considering itself not a business and perhaps the thought that "we don't need to sell" or "we shouldn't be selling." It is time to break out from that mindset! In today's world with the changes in the marketplace, it is no time to be timid. There is a lot to be learned from the for-profit sector. This is especially true when considering communications and marketing.

For nonprofit and social enterprise organizations, communication is important as there are multiple messages to be delivered and even more stakeholders who are involved. A for-profit only needs to consider its customers and shareholders in its communications. They care about the government and society to some degree, but mostly in relation to how those communications will impact their customer and their shareholders. For nonprofit and social enterprises, communications need to be managed for the clients that it serves, potentially there are multiple types of clients. It has donors, funders through grants, potentially also investors, volunteers, the government potentially is a funder making it a critical stakeholder. Managing all of these relationships and communication strategies is complex.

This chapter will focus on how to do this well and how to nuance a nonprofit or social enterprise's marketing strategy.

1. Marketing Mix (The 4 Ps of Marketing)

Marketing is everything that an organization does in order to get its offering to the customer to create an action (usually a purchase). The marketing mix that achieves this includes the 4 Ps of marketing:

- **Product:** What are you offering or making available? This is the offering which is typically a product or service that is designed to meet the customer's needs.

- **Price:** What will be charged for the offering? There are pricing strategies that can come into play to maximize profit or to maximize the volume or market share that an organization has.

- **Place:** Where can people get this? This is the distribution network and supply chain that is associated with making the offering available.

- **Promotion:** How will people find out about this and be interested in it? Promotion is what people typically assume is marketing, but the entire strategy needs to work together.

Together these four pieces of the puzzle add value to the customer and ensure that the right offering is at the right price, in the right time and place, and the customer will be aware of it.

Table 1
Marketing Mix Comparison

Marketing Mix	For-Profit	Social Initiatives
Product	Product, service, program, membership, events	Product, service, program, membership, events
Price	Maximize total profits	Maximize impact with a financial return
Place	Established supply chain, best practices	Nonestablished supply chains
Promotion	Fewer target markets	More target markets

2. How Is Marketing Different for a Social Initiative?

Typically there is a marketing mix that is designed for each customer type to which an organization is trying to appeal. With nonprofits and social enterprises having so many audiences in comparison to a for-profit, this means that more work and attention needs to be paid to this area. However, in each area of the marketing mix there are nuances as well:

- **Product:** Social initiatives have a wider range of offerings available to them and that continue to be explored including programs, memberships, and events.

- **Price:** Unlike a for-profit, a social initiative also is responsible for creating as large of a social impact as possible. In fact, this takes priority over the financial returns. But sustainability is always needed.

- **Place:** For-profits have been established with existing scale and infrastructure for their supply chains and distribution models. Social initiatives are often relatively new, exploring how to scale and if this is even viable, and are building their infrastructure which creates limitations on existing distribution capabilities. Another point is that social initiatives often serve geographical areas that are not financially attractive to for-profits, indicating that the infrastructure to serve those areas is at a higher cost with lower financial returns. Another supply chain that is not established is reverse logistics, which is the returns, defects, and recycling of products that have gone through or have gone through the supply chain. Social initiatives are involved in this part of the supply chain as it has an ecological impact as well as having a lower price point. A good example would be produce from a farm that does not meet the visual standards of a grocery store; it could be used at a soup kitchen in its soup. The concept of reverse logistics has evolved over the last two decades.

- **Promotion:** There are simply more groups to communicate with when it comes to social enterprises. For-profits need to focus on customers and shareholders with everyone else being secondary. For nonprofits and social enterprises, there is a lot more at stake with the secondary audiences. Governments and other organizations might be funders or volunteers. Potential donors and volunteers are a much larger audience than just investors to be concerned with (which social initiatives also care about). Social initiatives have to communicate to clients, investors, governments, charities, sponsors, donors, volunteers, and anyone who is a potential to be any of these in the future.

With all of these differences, it would initially appear that this is too much of an uphill battle to consider. A huge advantage in all of this work is that there is a keen sense of the need to partner between the social enterprises themselves and with government.

2.1 Marketing Partnerships for Social Enterprises

Partnerships are a key part of the marketing strategy that allow social enterprises to be competitive. For-profits also partner in their marketing for a strategic advantage, but never is it a point of necessity.

For social enterprises, leveraging partnerships throughout the entire marketing mix can have a significant advantage. It is a good idea to actively be thinking about what types of partnerships are needed and how to create these partnerships.

- **Product:** A social enterprise can partner with another social enterprise so that the collective offering is more appealing.

- **Price:** A social enterprise can partner with a corporation through a corporate social responsibility initiative, or with a foundation/ donor base to make an offering affordable through a subsidy or full sponsorship.

- **Place:** Social enterprises need to work together to build supply chains that allow them to scale. They need to work together when they jointly serve an area that is underserved or less accessible.

- **Promotion:** Social enterprises can partner together to reach any of their mutual audiences. As there are so many audiences to reach, partnering allows them to pool their marketing resources for joint advertising, promotion, or events. Corporate social responsibility is a good way to leverage a corporation's support and skills.

If marketing is critical to a social enterprise's success, and partnerships are critical to a social enterprise's marketing mix, it is fair to say that partnerships are critical for social enterprises.

2.2 Product: Social initiative offerings

What we already know:

- A product is the offering or what you are making available. In for-profits, an offering is typically a product or service that is designed to meet the customer's needs.

- Social enterprises have a wider range of offerings available to them and that continue to be explored including products, services, programs, memberships, and events.

- A social enterprise can partner with another social enterprise so that the collective offering is more appealing.

Offerings are above and beyond the normal fundraising and grants that a nonprofit might utilize. These are the new options that are available and being explored.

Creating a product or service that is for sale is the most commonly thought of business model. This can be used by a social enterprise.

But what makes it a social enterprise if the organization is simply selling a product?

For it to be a social initiative, the main focus of the organization needs to be making a social impact while creating a financial return. So when selling a product, it would have to adjust the business model to ensure a social impact was being made. Some ways to do this would include the following:

- Creating opportunities for employment for marginalized individuals or people who would otherwise not have employment.

- Having a pricing model so that customers paying a market price were subsidizing the clients who could not afford it.

- Focusing on the way that the product is manufactured or the service is delivered, by it being fair trade or decreasing the ecological impact that the product or service has on the environment.

- The organization is a nonprofit and the sale of a product or service is simply a fundraiser to support the other part of the organization.

Raw Carrot

Raw Carrot is a manufacturer of healthy soups that hires marginalized individuals in a rural community who would otherwise not be provided with skills training or a living wage. The ingredients for the soups are sourced locally and in partnership with the farmers in the region. The soups are sold through community groups, at fairs, and even through healthcare systems as they are organic and healthy.

Furniture Bank

Furniture Bank is an organization that picks up used furniture for a fee and then makes this used furniture available to people who cannot afford to furnish their homes after paying for their food and shelter. The clients are able to come to a large warehouse and select furniture at no cost, unless they require delivery. Furniture Bank is financially sustainable through the income from the deliveries and is able to provide a significant social impact acting as a furniture brokerage.

These examples are not exhaustive and social enterprises are continuing to experiment as to how social outcomes can be achieved creatively.

The key to creating a product or service as a social enterprise is to clearly understand how your offering is different from other nonprofits and social enterprises, but for-profit entities cannot be overlooked. In fact, it is a good idea to do a positioning chart to compare quality and price to the competition.

2.3 Programs

Programs are a creative way to connect to for-profit organizations' existing operations, while providing a social impact elsewhere.

Mealshare

Mealshare is a program where restaurants can identify a menu item that will provide a complimentary meal to a person in need. The price of the menu item takes into account the social impact and Mealshare connects with the organizations that deliver the meal. Mealshare doesn't directly perform a product or service, but instead has created a program that is financially sustainable and allows for the social impact to happen.

2.4 Memberships/subscriptions

Memberships and subscriptions are not the sole territory of social enterprises, but they are something that is used extensively due to the importance of engaging with people who care about a specific cause.

There are a few advantages to considering a membership or subscription model:

- By having a membership or subscription, people are able to actively indicate that they care and are contributing to this cause. This increases the chance that they would be willing to donate or volunteer for the cause.

- By being connected, you are able to regularly communicate with this audience through emails, mailouts, or during face-to-face activities. This helps to keep the cause and your organization top of mind.

The key is to build the community and to be able to provide consistent value to grow the membership and ensure that there is retention. The most common model for this is a Chamber of Commerce or an association, but new memberships and subscriptions continue to pop up.

Resource Church

A faith community had grown to a size where they had multiple ministers and were gathering a tremendous number of resources for services on Sunday mornings. They realized that some faith communities were not able to afford a full-time minister, yet wanted access to quality services. They made their resources available and provided monthly coaching on how to implement them on a monthly subscription.

2.5 Events

Events are utilized by for-profits often for brand awareness marketing, whereas nonprofits and social enterprises are able to use them for marketing, revenue generation, and volunteer recruitment.

Open Mic Showcase

A social enterprise was providing youth with skills training and providing a space to do Open Mic once a month. In order to support the programming that was involved, it asked the youth if they'd be interested in doing an Open Mic Showcase for the community. The youth were immediately excited about the opportunity to learn how to run an event, and a local event company volunteered its time to help with the process. Tickets were sold to the Showcase which would allow for the program to run throughout the rest of the year.

3. Price: Social Enterprise Revenue Generation Sources

What we already know about price:

- The price is what will be charged for the offering. There are pricing strategies that can come into play to maximize profit or to maximize the volume or market share that an organization has.

- Unlike a for-profit, a social enterprise also is responsible for creating as large of a social impact as possible. In fact, this takes priority over the financial returns.

- A social enterprise can partner with a corporation through a corporate social responsibility initiative or with a foundation/donor base to make an offering affordable.

Social enterprises are becoming more and more commonplace. That also means that we have more and more social innovators coming up with creative ways to generate revenue.

The old ideals of being 100 percent grant funded, or self-sufficient through donations, is gone. With government funding constantly being cut, disposable income declining, and the cost of doing business rising, social enterprises and nonprofits have to be more competitive and revenue seeking than ever before.

What are some pricing ideas? How can a nonprofit organization or social enterprise start to achieve revenue from multiple sources?

3.1 Fee for service (or product)

This is one of the simplest and best understood ways to generate revenue. It is providing a product or service to your customers that they are willing to pay for, or for which someone is willing to subsidize the fees or sponsor the service.

The fee for service model appears easy, but for many social enterprises and nonprofit organizations this can be a challenge as —

- the customers may be willing to pay, but unable to pay;

- the amount that the customers are able to pay does not pay for the cost of delivering the product or service; or

- it could be that beginning to charge for something that was historically free is difficult (for both the customers and also the staff of the organization).

Ideally if you are able to provide something for a price, and if that price is more than how much it costs to deliver, it is a sustainable revenue model.

Foodshare

The overall Foodshare model is to provide quality, local food, at a fair or low price to people. It bundles up food from farmers around urban areas, creates a bag of food that is at a fair or low price, and delivers to a pickup center to save on the distribution costs. Families pick up their bags of fruit and vegetables once a week and pay a fee for this service. This service can be operated on a subscription basis so no inventory is required as purchases match sales.

3.2 Cooperative/membership

One of the oldest forms of social enterprise is a cooperative model: either a for-profit or nonprofit organization owned by its members. Great examples include a farmers' cooperative, but even Costco acts as a cooperative with membership fees being a significant portion of their income. All Chambers of Commerce, associations, and Boards of Trade leverage membership fees to generate income.

The main challenge here is to ensure that your members get value out of being a member of your organization. With a farmers' cooperative, it should sell more produce or be able to get food at a lower price. For a Chamber of Commerce, it should have more business or learn something.

NewScoop YYZ

NewScoop YYZ is a cooperative that has been designed to bring together likeminded people to gather social justice stories and promote the sector, while providing content to the entire collective. It charges a membership fee and offers regular access to its content. It formed as a cooperative as it is all about everyone being together and caring about the same things.

3.3 Cross-compensation (partially/ fully subsidized models)

This is where the profits from one target market allow the organization to subsidize another target market to make it possible to serve them. Having two target markets is something that most organizations handle, but it can often be more challenging as the two target markets are potentially even more diverse including a different location, different needs, and different expectations.

You will need to ask yourself:

- Do both target markets need the same thing?
- Do the same things matter to them?
- Will different expectations be outlined?

- Will communication and marketing be different?
- Are there other ways your organization will need to adapt to having two distinct target markets?

Lytton Park Summer Camps

Lytton Park Summer Camps provides sports training and activities for children from 5 to 14 years of age. Often the facilities are located in affluent neighborhoods where tennis courts, soccer fields, and other amenities are widely available. Many of the facilities are at private schools. One target market is the affluent families in these neighborhoods and the children who go to the private schools for summer support. However, from the start it was recognized that many families in the neighborhood could not afford the camps and often had two working parents. The founders decided to provide space for these children and subsidize their spots.

3.4 Skills development

Skills development social enterprises act exactly like any other organization in its chosen industry, except that it specifically hires marginalized individuals who are having a difficult time getting jobs skills.

Examples of organizations that do this are in all sectors from restaurants, to manufacturing, to transportation and logistics, to services.

Gozie's Bread

Gozie's Bread is a bakery that hires ex-convicts and helps them get food preparation experience and certification for future employment opportunities. The location is away from the neighborhood where they would have previously been in trouble, and the training is both therapeutic and helpful in getting future employment.

3.5 Market intermediary/broker

A market intermediary/broker is where the social enterprise allows access to a new market through additional marketing, administration, distribution networks, or relationships.

3.6 Marketing

If an organization goes out of its way to market a product or service, it reduces the overhead and overall costs for the providing organization. These marketing expenses can allow for volume discounts for the marketing organization and a huge benefit for the organizations to which this is marketed. Buying groups are an example of this.

Buying United

The United Church realized, with thousands of churches buying similar products and services, that there was an advantage of having a single organization that negotiated pricing, performed due diligence, and then promoted these offerings in the language of the churches. It was quickly able to provide discounts on printing, supplies, and technology, and allow the church budgets to go further.

3.7 Administration

Performing the administration for another organization is common in the for-profit world with bookkeepers, accountants, consultants, virtual assistants, and other professional services being widely available. Doing this on a social enterprise basis is also possible and is beneficial when considering the governance and administrative differences of nonprofits and social enterprises.

Tides

Tides is an organization that provides a shared platform. This means that organizations don't have to register their own organizations, but can use the legal envelope of Tides until it has proven that it is something that is a going concern or is financially sustainable. The additional services include administration, management support, insurance, bookkeeping, and many others. Tides asks for a fixed percentage of the total revenue of the organizations in order to perform this role.

3.8 Distribution networks

Distribution is a huge cost for any organization needing to get its offering to its customers. If an organization is able to have access or streamline this, a huge value is provided. This could include a fulfillment center where the organization manages the products for multiple nonprofits or social enterprises or it could facilitate logistics shipments through a warehouse or direct to the customers (drop shipping).

Techsoup

Techsoup advocates for donated or substantially discounted software products from some of the largest software providers. These donated software products are then provided to nonprofit organizations that are considered eligible by the software providers. Techsoup charges an administrative fee to nonprofit organizations to account for it managing this process. This allows for a significant impact to the nonprofits while allowing Techsoup to grow and remain financially sustainable.

3.9 Relationships

Tapping into existing networks and relationships doesn't seem like a natural way to build a social enterprise, but relationships are the most valuable thing to have. Connecting people who need something to people who have something is critical. Social enterprises continue to look for ways to tap into this.

MAS Consulting

MAS Consulting offers pro bono consulting services to nonprofit organizations that need executive coaching, technology consulting, HR consulting, or a wide variety of other services. It actively seeks retired consultants that wish to give to the sector and then promote their services with nonprofit organizations. Although there is no fixed fee and the services are technically pro bono, organizations are asked to donate something to the administration of the organization in order to continue this work.

3.10 Sponsorship or corporate social responsibility

Are there opportunities to work with organizations or a volunteer base that provides value to your organization by being involved with your social enterprise or nonprofit organization? For example:

- Is there a team-building opportunity to volunteer time?

- Is donating to your cause something that the other organization could speak about in their marketing to customers?

- Is donating to your cause something that they could speak to their employees about?

- Is there another benefit that you could provide to them?

KPMG Consulting

KPMG, a consulting organization, volunteers its staff time to help nonprofits in their consulting or financial projects. This allows the consulting firm to give back, but also motivates the employees as they are part of making a positive difference.

3.11 Blended models

Finally, there are the blended models. For example, you don't have to only do sponsorships or sell products. You could find a sponsor to subsidize some of the products that you sell.

With grants, donations, and various revenue streams available, most social enterprises no longer rely on simply one source of income in order to remain viable. In fact, most will incorporate as many income streams as possible.

Depending on the sector and geographical location, there will be a tendency towards one source of income or another.

For example, in the United States, the healthcare system is private with nonprofit healthcare facilities applying for grants, seeking donations, but also charging fees for service. In Canada, the majority of the healthcare facilities receive a large percentage of their income from government grants, but they still actively apply for grants, seek donations, and charge for additional services including private rooms.

Another example is the difference between a farmers' market that is primarily a fee-for-service organization with some grant money, and an arts center which is run with a larger percentage of grants, donations, and sales.

Relying on only one source of income exposes an organization to risk. Nowadays and moving forward, diversified income streams for social enterprises are and will be the norm.

4. Place: Social Enterprise Distribution Models

What we already know about distribution models and social enterprise:

- Place is where people can get whatever you are offering. This is the distribution network and supply chain that is associated with making the offering available.

- For-profits have been established, often, with existing scale and infrastructure for their supply chains and distribution models. Social enterprises are relatively new, exploring how to scale and if this is even viable, and are building their infrastructure which creates limitations on existing distribution capabilities.

- Social enterprises often serve geographic areas that are not financially attractive to for-profits, indicating that the infrastructure to serve those areas is likely at a higher cost with lower financial return.

- Social enterprises need to work together to build supply chains that allow them to scale. They need to work together when they jointly serve an area that is underserved or less accessible.

- Distribution is all about supply chains. A supply chain is all of the steps to deliver a product or service to a customer from sourcing from suppliers to getting it to the customers at the right time and right place. Social enterprises need to be building new supply chains, collaborative distribution models, and to explore new ways of delivery. Supply chain and distribution are some of the largest barriers to the growth of the social enterprise sector.

- Distribution can include different ways to get it to the customer including:

  - Traditional retail or consignment

  - Fulfillment center

  - Drop shipping

  - Online stores

  - Commission or referral fees

There is a large movement to consider social procurement, the process of purchasing from socially responsible organizations. This is especially prevalent amongst governments and large nonprofit organizations.

Although the demand is there for social procurement, there are few social enterprises that have the scale and capability to deliver on some of these large procurement contracts that are being made available.

Distribution networks are one of the critical factors to helping the supply side grow.

4.1 Direct to client

Social enterprises often sell directly to clients. That is where the social enterprise is the direct or main point of contact interacting with the end client of the offering.

This makes a lot of sense for social enterprises, as they have created their offering in order to make a social or ecological impact. Why wouldn't they want to see their impact firsthand?

There are some major advantages of being direct to client for a social enterprise:

- The direct knowledge the impact occurred.

- The immediate feedback from the end client.

- The ability to better tell the story for donations and volunteers based on the direct impact.

Bereavement Centre

A church in a suburb of Montreal gathered together partners in palliative care and a funeral home in order to support the people in the neighborhood going through the grieving process. This type of work is extremely emotional and takes a personal approach. Being direct with the clients allows it to make a huge impact and be as supportive as possible.

4.2 Resellers/channel partners

Resellers and channel partners are organizations that make your offering available to their clients. They are a way to reach a larger client base and take advantage of their local presence.

Some advantages of having resellers/channel partners include:

- The organization is present over a much larger geographic area.

- The organization is able to reach and help a larger number of people.

- The organization is able to keep its infrastructure and fixed costs lower which helps with financial sustainability and resilience.

4.3 Overseas partnerships

Although there are a lot of social causes that need addressing in North America, there are even more overseas in developing countries where the standard of living, on average, is dramatically lower. There are a larger number of people living in poverty as there is a huge income gap and there are other challenges including human rights and war ravaged areas.

There are many organizations that wish to make a difference overseas, but realize that it doesn't make sense for them to have operations internationally as they don't know the language, culture, or have the connections to make it successful. In these cases, it makes sense to partner with organizations that are already established in these countries and simply need support in order to make a bigger impact.

Red Cross

Red Cross has partnership organizations in every single country in the world. It needs to as it is designed to react to any large scale emergency from a natural disaster to a terrorist attack. It doesn't make logistical sense for Red Cross to have an office in each country, but it does make sense to build relationships in each country to mobilize existing infrastructure when needed.

4.4 Online store/direct access using technology

Technology continues to change the world in unexpected and new ways. In supply chain and distribution networks, it allows organizations to connect with their end clients more easily without a physical presence.

Technology also allows for things to be delivered in new ways including some of these examples:

- People can access a nurse via a 1-800 number to determine if they need to go to a doctor or hospital.

- People can purchase handcrafted items from Africa to support people in those communities.

- People can access support for mental illness or abuse via helplines.

As technology continues to advance and is more accessible to people, the ways in which social enterprise can tap into these opportunities will help to scale the support available.

5. Promotion of a Social Enterprise

What we already know about promotion and social enterprise:

- Promotion is the way in which people will find out about the enterprise and be interested in it.

- Promotion is what people typically assume is marketing, but the entire strategy needs to work together.

- Promotion is only part of marketing.

- Social enterprises have more people to communicate with and engage.

- Social enterprises can partner together to reach their mutual audiences. As there are so many audiences to reach, this allows them to pool their marketing resources.

- Promotion is what happens now that we have our offering, have our pricing, and understand how our offering will get to the customer (the distribution or place). Once all of that is figured out, we need to get awareness of what we are doing out there. This can include the following methods:

  - Advertising

  - Public relations

  - Sales team and channel partner sales

  - Promotions of various types

  - Marketing, whether direct, online, or guerilla

The remainder of this chapter will be dedicated to digging deeper into these topics.

5.1 Advertising

Advertising is the type of promotion that is most readily apparent to society. When people think of how to get awareness for a product or service, they almost immediately think of mainstream media that they are regularly exposed to including television, radio, newspaper, transit, magazines, online advertising, signage, and the like.

Each type of advertising is designed for different purposes, and social enterprises should be careful in selecting which ones are the best for them. In general it is good to think about the reach of each medium, the target audience the medium will reach, and the response rate based on the information shared and duration of the message.

5.1a Television

Television is one of the widest reaching mediums. There are also local stations and online television options. Television is typically one of the most expensive options due to its reach, but for social enterprises this is not often necessary unless the offering is something that could be taken advantage of on the same scale.

World Vision

World Vision is one of the most commonly remembered nonprofits that leverages television advertising. It has been doing television advertising for decades showing families and children that it supports in developing countries. This medium makes sense for World Vision as people can donate across the country online or by calling. It has set up its organization to use this method of generating awareness.

5.1b Radio

Radio is surprisingly effective and is great for a local market. Unfortunately the audience is dropping as more people prefer to use their own music rather than have to listen to advertising or repetitive music. The cost remains low, although during peak listening hours, there can be premiums. Most radio stations have a lot of information about their listening demographics to help with deciding where the best value might be. If you partner with one of their contests or promotions, you can get even more bang for your buck.

5.1c Newspapers

Newspapers continue to be a popular way to get the latest news with both physical newspapers and online news. However, print advertising rates are decreasing as there is competition with online advertising which also provides live news feeds. This is an increasingly cost effective way to reach a local market.

Canadian Cancer Society

A unique way to leverage advertising is to proactively thank your sponsors and donors. The Canadian Cancer Society and other nonprofits often thank their major sponsors and donors using full-page advertising to recognize those contributors. This is a way to generate awareness with prospective donors while recognizing the existing contributors at the same time.

5.1d Magazines

Magazines often have extremely niche readerships and have a long life as they are often passed on. Niche magazines allow the social enterprise to ensure that very specific types of people become aware.

United Church Foundation

The United Church Foundation advertises heavily in the *UCObserver* Magazine. It recognizes that more than 100,000 people read the monthly magazine and almost all of these people could be interested in a donation to the foundation that makes many of the interesting initiatives possible.

5.1e Billboards and transit advertising

Signage is an extremely local approach that can often generate an immediate response. This is a great medium for neighborhood-based social enterprises that only need people around them to know about them. For transit, this would target people who can't drive or have decided not to drive including students who might have a car or license. Billboard advertising is often for people who are driving and typically commuting for work.

Colleges

Most urban transit lines have advertising that is specifically geared to students or people who might want to upgrade their résumé with a college degree or diploma.

5.1f Online advertising

Online advertising is taking an increasing amount of most organizations' marketing budgets as this advertising proves more and more effective. Initially there were banner ads, e-newsletter ads, and some basic placement advertising online. But with big data and an increasing amount of information about online consumer behavior, online advertising is becoming more complex and strategic. Here are some of the basic forms:

- Pay-per-click ads are where you only pay for the advertising once a consumer clicks on the ad that is either on a search engine or within a website. As this advertising is based on interest levels (the consumer has clicked on the ad) it can vary from a few pennies to a few dollars at a time. It is important that the landing pages that these links go to are compelling and have the information that has been indicated in the advertisement to take advantage of this.

- Pop-ups are when the advertisement is in a new window that covers the webpage that the consumer is currently viewing. In order to close the advertisement the consumer must physically click on the ad.

- Placement (specific spots for ads) is still in existence on many websites and e-newsletters, specifically when they are industry related or niche. Most search engines use pay-per-click or cost-per-action.

- Social media advertising is when the advertisement is embedded in a social media tool that the consumer regularly uses such as Facebook or LinkedIn. This can be placement ads or pay-per-click, but is unique in that the social media accounts are able to track usage and other behaviors in order to better customize the advertisements.

In general, what you need to think about when considering your advertising program:

- Is your target client or stakeholder likely to see this medium of advertising?

- How many times would he or she have to see it to make a difference?

- Can you afford this?

- How many people who aren't your target are you paying to get in front of?

- Will you have a larger benefit to your social enterprise than the cost of doing this form of advertising?

- Is there a better way to get this same result?

Use the online resources on the download kit to answer these questions and create your advertising program.

5.2 Public relations

Public relations is one of the most underrated ways to generate awareness about your organization. Public relations is when the existing news media talks about your organization, as it is newsworthy. Typically the most effective message is the story, in either print, video, or audio. This could be you being talked about in newspaper or magazine articles, or you as a guest speaker on the radio, or you being interviewed on television.

There are a few great reasons to use this rather than advertising:

- It is more credible. People are much more likely to believe the claims of an organization if it is in the news rather than in an advertisement.

- It is free. Other than the time and work to put together a media release and work with the press, there is no other cost.

The main challenges include:

- It isn't guaranteed. You might do a lot of upfront work trying to generate some press and no media will be interested in your story.

- You lose control of the message. Part of being interviewed by any medium is that they need to put their own slant on it. Often this means digging into the story deeper, telling multiple angles about the story, and that the organization that generates the interest in the story is not able to review it prior to it being live or printed. Sometimes it is just a small part of the interview that is in the medium which could distort the organization's intended message.

With the advantages and disadvantages of public relations in mind, the following are different approaches to generate the media's interest.

5.2a Events

Events are a great reason to reach out to the press. You might have a celebrity present or it might be something that the press wants to tell people about in advance. Visuals are usually appealing and there are multiple people for them to interview. Videos with a celebrity and a client are the most impactful.

The main challenge is that events have a finite opportunity of time to capture. If there is an emergency or better story during the same window, the event may not get the visibility you hoped for.

5.2b New information

Is there something new that is happening in your sector that is interesting that you are involved in? The media could look at this as a chance to educate the population, and let them know about something that might not normally be on the radar, or to highlight this change in case it will affect a large portion of the population. This could be a success story or the outcome that has been achieved by the organization.

The main challenge is to still showcase your organization while the media will be more interested in the new information.

5.2c Leveraging a trend

Is there a topic that is already in the news that your organization is doing something about, could get involved in somehow, or has a different viewpoint on? If the media is already featuring a type of story, this is your chance to leverage this. Become known as an expert for the media to reach out to.

The main challenge here is ensuring that the viewpoint that you are taking is in fact different. If there is a lot of news about a particular topic, it is a narrow window before the media stops covering that story.

5.2d Network and build relationships

When all else fails, focus on building your relationships with the media. Understand what types of news they are looking for, understand their scheduling and when stories might be needed, and finally, be patient as building these relationships takes time.

Center for Social Innovation

The Center for Social Innovation is both a coworking space as well as a network of social entrepreneurs based in New York City and Toronto. As the buzzword "social innovation" continues to grow in usage, the Center for Social Innovation showcases its new members who had great ideas and it continues to feed information about the social sector to the media. By doing this over time it has become the go-to resource for the media for social innovation or social enterprise quotations and ideas.

5.3 Sales team and channel partner sales

You don't have to do all of the marketing and awareness yourself. Having a sales team (internal or contracted) and channel partners to help scale up your efforts can be tremendously helpful. In fact, the larger the scale or the fundraising effort, the more important sales becomes in your overall marketing efforts.

For example, if you are fundraising for big gifts, such as more than $10,000, it would make sense to have a personal sales effort that campaigns for those larger donations.

The same applies that personal sales are critical when the sale is more than $2,000 as there is increased risk to the customer or client with the higher price tag. They will have more questions that are specific to their needs and benefits and will need them answered by an individual.

5.3a Sales team

A sales team is personnel who work for your organization or are directly contracted by your organization (as in a sales agency). This gives you more control over the sales force and visibility, but it also increases your overhead as you most likely would have both salaries and commission to pay.

The other alternative is to have volunteers as your salespeople. This is often leveraged in fundraising campaigns. Volunteers also have good contacts as sales leads through their friends, family, and extended networks.

5.3b Channel partner sales

A channel partner is another organization outside of your organization that does the sales or fundraising for you. As they don't work in your organization you don't have the additional overhead, however, you will have to share in your profit as a sales commission or a percentage of the margin is retained by the channel partner for generating the sale.

You don't have as much control over what they communicate and where they spend their time when speaking with customers, which often means that you have to create specific promotions for sales persons to incent them to focus on your organization.

5.4 Promotions of various types

Promotions are any incentive for either salespeople or the end consumers in order to entice activity sooner rather than at a later date.

5.4a Customer promotions

Most customer promotions either add more value to the offering or offer a pricing incentive. Here are some examples:

- Coupons
- Price discounts
- Bundling
- Promotional products
- Trials

5.4b Fundraising promotions

Unlike product- or service-related promotions, fundraising promotions are focused on the customer donating today or a specific amount. Here are some examples:

- Recognition
- Matching funds
- Matching funds after a minimum
- Promotional products

United Way Corporate Matching

United Way works closely with corporations to raise funds during corporation fundraising events for the month of October. Part of the campaign is to ask employees to donate monthly from their paychecks to United Way. The other is to negotiate with the corporations that they will match employee donations if the annual donation is more than $1,000. This incents the employees to hit the minimum matching donation threshold if they are close to it, and allows the corporation to report and discuss the positive social impact they are making.

5.4c Sales promotions

A sales promotion is any incentive that is created for a client to purchase or for a sales person to sell. The most recognizable sales promotions are a sale price, rebates, coupons, or contest for clients to buy. However, sales promotions are often designed for either the sales team or the channel partners to focus on specific messaging that the organization is interested in prioritizing. Here are some examples:

- Trips or other prizing for the best salespeople.
- Additional commissions for selling a specific product or service.
- Recognition of the best salespeople through awards or prizes.
- Certification or thank-you letter to the channel partners.
- Referral discounts to the channel partners.

The important thing to learn in promotions is that they are designed to incent stakeholders that represent your organization and have an impact on your success.

5.5 Other Marketing Strategies

5.5a Direct marketing

Direct marketing is about ensuring that your message is literally delivered to the audience you want to see it. This can be done through:

- Fliers/efliers
- Direct mail
- Email
- Newsletters
- Door-to-door sales
- Thank-you letters

All of this can also be referred to as junk mail or spam. It is direct and yet it is often considered ineffective as so many direct messages are discarded by the intended audience.

However, "success" comes when there is a positive benefit for your efforts. In the case of direct marketing, although only a small percentage of direct marketing material is actually viewed, if 2 percent of the audience actually does the action that was intended it might be a success.

In fact, many times it is the direct marketing efforts that convert the sale. Increasingly this is due to email because of the low cost of doing this. But don't underestimate the power of getting something physical in the mail!

Heart Foundation

Annually, the Heart Foundation sends thank-you letters to all of its donors from the year with an added ask for additional pledge money. This is a tangible thanks, and it is packaged with asking for additional funds. The donors recognize the Heart Foundation, appreciate the recognition, and then a percentage decide to give even more.

5.5b Online marketing

If you aren't doing online marketing, you are missing out! It is now close to a mandatory part of any business and marketing plan. And it can give your organization a huge boost.

Being found by your audience is the most important thing. But there is so much online, how do you become higher ranked so that people can find you more easily on search engines?

Search Engine Optimization (SEO) has become the art around how to do this. Search engines, such as Google, Bing, YouTube, and Yahoo!, create their own formulas to decipher if a website or webpage is the best on a specific topic. Often it is a combination of using the right words, having a lot of content, and visuals. This formula changes frequently and varies for different search engines, but the end concept is that the search engines want to make sure that the best content for a search is found by their users.

For-profit organizations can spend a lot of time and money ensuring that they are at the top. They might even do this by paying for advertising. Nonprofits and social enterprises also need to be aware of this, as they can now have people be aware of them internationally and the opportunity to have even more of a reach.

The key thing to consider is giving the search engines what they are looking for: Good content for their users. Consider the following:

- **Content to read:** Do you have a lot of content? The number changes but you usually want more than 300 words per page as a minimum and that number seems to be increasing.

- **Content to see:** Are there visuals and are they related to the content?

- **Content to watch:** Do you have videos, especially stories by end users describing a benefit?

- **More content to find:** Are you referring the readers to more links that are related to the same content, that are good?

- **Quality content:** Are people commenting or sharing this on social media as they think others will benefit from it? Are people linking to your content?

- **New content:** How often is the content on your site changing or being updated?

In general, trying to provide quality content is the best way to move yourself and your organization up the ranks.

Social media is another great way to generate massive awareness online, and an active way to get people to know about you and your social impact.

The main social media platforms are Facebook, Twitter, and Instagram. They have discovered how to integrate with other platforms. They've made it easy to update them, they have communities, and they are extremely visual in their medium.

Social media also supports your search engine optimization through commenting and linking back to your web pages, which all helps you get found.

Videos are another way that people communicate online, and this is often the case for millennials. In fact, the second largest search engine in the world is YouTube, a video-hosting platform.

Videos have a way of being able to visualize and vocalize the message that you are trying to get across. This allows for them to go viral, as everyone wants to watch it as it can evoke an emotion. That is why for organizations that make a social impact, videos are a great way to tell clients' stories of how you have impacted them and get the word out about your offerings.

ALS Ice Bucket Challenge

In 2015, a phenomenon rolled across the world: The Ice Bucket Challenge launched by ALS. Famous people were challenged to dump an ice bucket over their heads, film it, post it online, and then challenge more of their friends to follow.

Within a few weeks almost the entire world's population had heard about the challenge and many had done it. The idea was that each person would donate money to ALS at the same time or, in some cases, to prevent themselves from having to do the challenge.

Not only did ALS raise a lot of money from this campaign, but the awareness surrounding the campaign and the cause increased dramatically.

5.5c Guerilla marketing

People are inundated with information. They are communicated with at almost every single part of the day. How do you break through the clutter?

Guerilla marketing is the unorthodox way of breaking through the clutter. It is doing things to generate awareness using brand new methods. Some examples of this include:

- Spontaneous dance parties or flash mobs
- Creating a fake advertisement or messaging
- April Fool's Day jokes
- Any other tactic that is used as a "fun"draiser

Of course, it is impossible to list all of the types of guerilla marketing as the definition of guerilla marketing is unorthodox ways. So there will continue to be guerilla marketing tactics invented.

Events can be unique and have a lot of opportunity to do inspiring things to make an impact. Most events leverage some type of guerilla marketing to get a point across:

- Activities for the event attendees to participate in physically (photo booths, games)
- Lotteries, giveaways, or funny contests
- A surprise speaker or performer or some other surprise
- Any other way that an event attempts to be unique and stick out

NFL Breast Cancer Support

Sporting events are already in place and spend a tremendous amount of money to help entertain the attendees. One creative way that a breast cancer organization generated massive awareness was to partner with the NFL and make one week during October Breast Cancer week. Each team was encouraged to add some pink coloring to their outfits from socks to armbands to face paint. The fields and signage also showed the ribbon. Tapping into an existing event and leveraging it as a third party benefited both parties despite it at first appearing unrelated.

Celebrities are always a good approach to gain attention. You are more likely to have people attend events, get good press, and have general interest when a celebrity is onboard.

Often, celebrities also believe that it is part of their responsibility to take on this role and use their popularity to make a social impact. Large companies also leverage celebrity sponsorships, so this could be a way to connect with large organizations as well. Celebrities and sports stars are committed to sponsors to make a number of appearances during the contract. Ask!

The challenge is in reaching them and then ensuring that they are a good fit with your cause. You definitely don't want to have a celebrity endorsement from someone who is either not a good fit or someone who doesn't understand your work.

Grammy Awards Support

Each year the Grammys support a different cause in order to make a social impact. Often any sort of prizing that is given out financially is also to a charity. This national awareness as well as being supported by so many celebrities often propels these charities forward.

Also, word of mouth: Get people talking about it! Anything that you can do that starts people talking about you, especially on social media, is a good thing.

Doing things differently to get people's attention is important. The second part is thinking about how to get that awareness and turn it into something more. What is that second stage? What else do you have to do to get there?

Kaepernick

In 2016, the famous NFL quarterback, Kaepernick, protested on behalf of Black Lives Matter by remaining seated during the American national anthem.

The following week there was an outrage. People talked about his stance and whether or not it was effective or appropriate. In the end, it was determined that if the end result is getting people to talk about it, then it certainly was successful.

See the download kit included with this book for a template of an advertising plan to get you started on these aspects of your initiative.

CHAPTER 5
YOUR TEAM

1. Recruit Volunteers, Staff, and Everyone in Between

Having the right people is the most important part of any initiative. In social enterprise and nonprofit there is no difference; in fact, it is often even more important based on the slim budgets and the vital work that needs to be done.

To do this well, it is critical to find great people and keep them!

The advantage when finding and keeping these great people is that a nonprofit or social enterprise is doing dynamic work which is attractive to many people. The disadvantage is that typically the roles you are offering are voluntary and there are many nonprofits and social enterprises looking for the same people who are willing to give their time.

Most nonprofits and social enterprises have a variety of different roles. This is in part due to the fact that there is so much work to get done, but also with the understanding that a variety of roles opens up how many people can be a part of it.

If all of the roles required full-time, dedicated volunteers, the number of eligible people would dramatically decline. By offering variety you allow volunteers to be minimally to fully involved.

Here are some examples of roles that a nonprofit or social enterprise might need:

- Management and support
- Board of directors
- Patrons
- Volunteer boards of advisors
- Committees
- Ambassadors and community teams
- Peers
- Mentors (general and specific) and coaches (general and specific)
- Paid advisors

To lay the foundations of a growing organization, there needs to be people to support the infrastructure. Delegation is the key.

2. Define Roles, Recruit, Train, Retain, and Recognize!

Finding and keeping great people is the difference between a good and great organization. Understanding this and putting the pieces in place is an important step.

The key pieces to think about include:

- **Define:** What will the roles and their responsibilities be? Develop position descriptions.
- **Recruit:** How will you go about the process of attracting candidates and selecting the right ones?

- **Train:** Orient the resources and support team members to realize their optimal potential.

- **Retain:** Do the work to keep your employees and volunteers.

- **Recognize:** Develop ways in which you highlight and provide benefits for your team's great work.

Managing human resources can be more complicated with the blend of both employees and volunteers. Not only do they behave and expect different things out of the relationship, but there is also a complicated interaction between employees and volunteers.

For example, one interesting dynamic is between the Board of Directors of a nonprofit and the Executive Director. The Executive Director is often the founder of the nonprofit and is heavily invested in the cause and future of the organization. He or she is deeply integrated in the daily operations and sometimes the sole employee of the organization. But it is the Board of Directors where approvals of larger expenses and future directions are made. This diffusion of the accountability from the responsibility can be frustrating for both parties.

To establish the team which is the core resource needed to execute the idea, there are steps to take, but you need to know how to take them, and resources to support these activities. This is all a lot of work! When first setting up your team, you should make a plan of who you need to spend the effort to recruit.

3. Who Is Your Team?

Based on your needs you can build this team over a period of time and may not require all members at once. Imagine trying to find and train all of these people at the same time. Recognize that for scalability and growth, it makes sense to be strategic and patient in building this foundation. Not to mention that financially it isn't feasible to scale all at once! Never forget that your most important resource is and always will be your people.

So who do you need? Who should you be considering and in what order?

3.1 Management and support team

The initial employee is the president (in a social enterprise) or an executive director (within a nonprofit). These are the people with the initial passion and drive to get the idea off the ground. They might have come up with the idea or had a personal experience with the issue they are addressing.

A core team member is one who is interested in social good and wants to participate with a group to define and solve a problem with a solution that will achieve measureable results for the parties impacted. The igniter is the person who starts the activity by talking to others who may have an interest and passion about participating in a group session. The members could meet on an informal basis to define the first steps.

Usually the first hire after the leader is a virtual assistant or a volunteer coordinator. Depending on finances this might start off as a few hours a week or a contract role.

After the start-up phase the core team of employees and volunteers will have been recruited to grow the organization to the next level or to maintain the existing operations in a sustainable way. As there is stability, there is often a need to grow the staffing infrastructure of the team. Additional key future contract team members might be:

- **Marketing:** A communications, marketing, sales, and media director responsible for building the brand name, revenue streams, and media messaging. The larger the organization, the more that this department and function will grow. The more funding that is raised by a nonprofit or social enterprise, the more positive impact will be created. Large hospital foundations typically have a majority of their staff working in this functional area.

- **Human resources:** A human resources and volunteer management director who will be responsible for employees, contractors, and volunteers and their recruitment, training, retention, and recognition. Having someone dedicated to the most important resource of the organization just makes sense. The number of people in this function could increase.

- **Strategy and partnerships:** A research and development role or partnership role will be responsible for product and project management, and partnership and supplier collaboration. This group would help support the executive director in future planning and helping to bring together the pieces that make this possible.

There are many other functional areas that would also evolve, similarly to a for-profit or other organization including finance, operations, and program teams.

3.2 Board of directors

The board will start as an operations board and over time transition to a governance board responsible for policy, governance, fiduciary matters, supervision of the management team, approving the strategic plan, approving major initiatives or expenditures, and opening doors to new relationships within the network. With this in mind, you are looking for multitalented individuals who can handle this responsibility while being flexible enough to work with.

Finding a board of directors that understands the new economy and social enterprise as a strategy to leverage in the nonprofit space is important.

Based on the importance of tapping into the board's network, it is good to have members of the board who are connected in almost any sector including corporate, government, academic, and others in the social sector (nonprofit, charities, social enterprise, foundations, etc.).

The board of directors for a charity or nonprofit should be volunteers. Liability insurance should be investigated and a plan purchased to ensure protection of the directors.

In the beginning a board of directors acts as an operations board. An operations board means that the team would aid in day-to-day tasks. They work closely with the executive director in helping to get the initiative off the ground. They most likely have a personal relationship with the founder of the organization and would have similar passion in the initiative. They would help with recruitment and fundraising, as well as meeting regularly to discuss future direction and the status updates of the growth. The meetings would be rather ad hoc at this stage and the full complement of board members may not yet be recruited.

Eventually the board would transition into a governance board which is no longer involved in the daily operations. This change will take some time as the responsibilities change to more oversight, strategic planning, policy, and decision-making.

At this point the board should be more structured and include the following roles:

- **Chair:** The board's leader who runs the meetings and might even have a tie-break voting power.

- **Vice Chair:** Support of the leader and a back-up for when the Chair is not available.

- **Secretary/Treasurer:** Records the notes of the meetings and ensures that the format is followed as well as documented.

- **Others:** There are often two to four other directors with various backgrounds to balance out the board.

Meetings would be organized on a regular time schedule of either monthly or quarterly, with an agenda and supporting material. Typically the meetings would be to review the progress of the organization but also to help the management in making strategic decisions on problems and opportunities.

3.3 Patrons

These are individuals who support the vision, mission, and objectives of the organization by lending their name, title, and organization. In some situations, you may ask for a letter or a testimonial comment or a video.

When launching the social initiative, just like with any start-up, it is important to build credibility. "Fake it 'til you make it" works for social organizations just as it does with a for-profit start-up. For-profits need to act like they are a bigger and more established business for larger potential customers to consider them. They might create fancy titles, use references from previous employers rather than just past customers, and try other tactics. For a social initiative, patrons want to be associated with winners and this image needs to be portrayed prior to all of the results being realized.

To have some of your first patrons it is important to start with existing relationships that you or your board of directors have. Provide any information about any successes that you have had to date. Based on the size of your organization, small success is something to celebrate. For example:

- Have you had an event that has drawn a large audience?

- Do you have stories of the clients that have received the social benefit? What did they say about the work that you are doing? Has it been on social media?

- Do you have other patrons or could your board provide support for why a new patron should be interested in formally supporting?

Individuals who wish to be a patron for the cause may not want to be active but support the cause by way of a video or text testimonial.

Growing this group is important to expand your network. Although the patrons are important in themselves, their network holds even more potential.

Quickly it becomes important to have a communication strategy with the patrons. This could be via either or both a newsletter or a semi-annual update of progress and achievements.

3.4 Volunteer board of advisors

Boards of advisors are a way to engage critical people into the strategic decisions without involving them in fiduciary duty. As they are not a formal board of directors they don't have the liability of making the decisions, but they are given the responsibility to be part of the process. See Sample 11 for how you might separate the expertise.

This is a great way to extend the voice to a larger audience to gain sales leads and referrals and get free advice on problems and opportunities.

Boards of advisors will give the organization a unique perspective. In the beginning stages the time to set this up and run these meetings may outweigh the benefits that are realized. When to set these up will be based on this delicate balance.

As the organization grows, having boards of advisors becomes more important as the management becomes further removed from the grassroots and more disconnected from the landscape.

Some types of advisory boards include:

- **Customers:** Having a group of customers that discusses their concerns and feedback directly to the organization helps it to be more responsive to the customers' needs.

- **Partners:** How do your partners like working with you? What could be improved? Also, with the partners meeting with each other through this forum there could be even more connections made. Simply being on the board of advisors could be a benefit of working with you.

Sample 11
Advisory Boards Detail

ADVISORY BOARDS

PAID ADVISORS

AREA	NAME	COMPANY	PHONE	EMAIL
Finance	John Willis	Company 1	555-4444	john@com1.com
Marketing	Sam Yu	Company 2	555-5555	sam@com2.com
Staffing	Elaine Heart	Company 3	555-6666	elaine@com3.com

VOLUNTEER ADVISORY BOARD — BUSINESS — Thurs. 7:30

AREA	NAME	COMPANY	PHONE	EMAIL

VOLUNTEER ADVISORY BOARD — CUSTOMERS — Tues. 7:30

AREA	NAME	COMPANY	PHONE	EMAIL

VOLUNTEER ADVISORY BOARD — TECHNICAL — Sat. 10:30

AREA	NAME	COMPANY	PHONE	EMAIL
Online-Finance	Joe Burns	n/a	555-1111	joe@comna.com
Networks	Tom Wang	First Bank	555-2222	tom@firstbank.com
Computers	Sarah John	Joe's Computers	555-3333	sarah@joescomp.com

Sample 11 — Continued

VOLUNTEER BOARD PROCESS STEPS

1. ID and recruit paid advisors; seek referrals where possible.

2. ID needs for volunteer advisory board(s) and define responsibilities: monthly meeting, two emails and two telephone responses per month. You may need more than one board, for example, business board (finance, marketing, technology, operations/production); subject matter board (health, nutrition, fitness, trainer); and a customer board (four or five customers with different perspectives).

3. Recruit through network and have them sign confidentiality/noncompetition agreement.

4. Organize and conduct first 20- to 25-minute meetings via Skype or Google Hangouts with two agenda items. Document discussion and decisions.

5. Add advisor names and ads on company website.

Owner Benefits of Advisory Boards

1. Free information and advice.

2. Sales leads and referrals.

3. Alliances/partnership/supplier/contractor/professionals leads and referrals.

4. Credibility to business — advisors shown on site/blog/newsletter/letterhead — helps re: suppliers, customers/prospects, and financial sources such as banks.

Benefits to Advisor (use in recruitment process)

1. Network with other advisors.

2. Company sends official letter to advisor's supervisor (or provides a testimonial) recognizing contribution.

3. Free ad on company website/blog/letterhead.

4. Opportunity to learn and socialize.

- **Volunteers:** How are the volunteers feeling? Are they being appreciated? Are there ideas percolating at the grassroots that could be implemented?

- **Business:** Specialists in areas such as marketing, finance, technology, and program development can add value from a different lens.

Each board of advisors should be composed of at least five individuals to ensure that there is diversity in the perspectives. Also, when the entire group agrees, this is something that is validated and should be considered immediately. The format is that a staff from the organization should listen and take notes. The advisors are encouraged to speak openly by providing input and suggestions to the organization.

Short and frequent meetings are recommended. One structure could be monthly meetings for only 25 minutes. To ensure that there is quality in the information from the advisors, it is recommended to only have one agenda item each month. These meetings don't always have to be face-to-face, and considering web conferencing or other technology solutions such as Skype or FaceTime is a good idea. There could be additional emails, but it is important to limit this and help keep down the time commitment of these volunteers. For example, a maximum of two emails and two phone calls per month.

3.5 Committees

Committees can be set up based on the people that can be recruited. Usually the first committee is marketing, to help grow the fundraising and recruitment of future volunteers. The executive director and staff typically would handle the other committee functions until the size permits otherwise. (See Sample 12.)

As the initiative grows in momentum and size, the number of committees will also increase. The names and objectives of committees will vary. Each should have a Chair and a Vice Chair as this not only ensures that there is responsibility, but this is seen as a benefit for some of the volunteers that could leverage these roles on their résumés. Often the committee is a combination of more regular volunteers and more ad hoc volunteers.

The following are committee suggestions and include some key responsibilities. Each would require development of policies, processes, forms, and procedures to include in an operations guide to help inform existing and new team members:

- **Marketing:** Communication is needed to grow the initiative. Communication is with existing and future customers, partners, volunteers, donors, employees, or patrons. This committee focuses on the messaging and all of the tactical ways to get the message out there. With online options expanding, this committee becomes more important and there is more work that needs to be done in this area.

- **Finance:** This committee focuses on financial support to ensure the financial viability of the organization. This would include financial planning, monitoring, and sourcing.

- **Human resources:** As recognized in this chapter, human resources have a lot of infrastructure work that is necessary to

Sample 12
Committees Details

The following sets out the terms of reference and position descriptions. For job postings both would be needed.

TERMS of REFERENCE: HUMAN RESOURCES AND VOLUNTEER MANAGEMENT

Committee Overview:

The committee members will reflect members of the community and/or have experience and/or interest in human resources and volunteer management.

- The committee will represent members from across the country, and different areas: urban, rural.
- Membership terms are two years, and can be renewed for one term (committee members will be expected to make best efforts to attend all committee meetings — min. 75% — and participate in at least one annual initiative).
- The Chair of the committee will be approved by the Board of Directors.

Purpose:

The primary purpose of this committee is to establish the management team and the volunteer team. The group is responsible for defining roles and responsibilities within the organization structure and its many volunteer needs. This includes developing descriptions and performance targets for the different management and volunteer positions; establishing and/or creating appropriate recruitment processes, training, and support; developing appropriate retention, recognition, and cultivation programs to ensure that we maximize people's potential and engagement.

Key Objectives:

- Define roles, responsibilities, performance targets, and document position descriptions for the overall organizational structure including board of directors, standing committees, advisory boards, committee champions, and ambassadors;
- Develop and deliver volunteer orientation, training sessions, and ongoing support networks, primarily online and webinar formats;
- Develop, implement, and evaluate employee and key volunteer retention, promotion, and recognition programs;
- Establish, maintain, and monitor the use of an employee and volunteer management manual to include policies, procedures, rules, and forms, etc.

Knowledge, Skills, Experience (or interest in learning):

- Some academic training or professional experience in volunteer and/or human resources management
- Experience in a volunteer role/capacity and within a nonprofit organization
- Excellent communication skills verbally and online and in writing

Time Commitment

Initially, the tasks outlined above will require considerable time until a team is recruited to perform sub tasks helping the champions. Most of this work can be performed by telephone, email, video conferencing etc., as decided by the team.

Once the core teams are recruited, the individual area plans established, and training and manuals are completed, the ongoing time requirement will significantly decline, with emphasis on retention and recognition of volunteers, as well as defining new roles for the organization.

Benefits

- Learning and applying new skills, methods, and approaches in volunteer management
- Networking with a wide variety of individuals across the country
- Recognition by the organization by way of a letter to a supervisor or a letter outlining contributions to be included in a career portfolio and resume, or a testimonial to the business
- Recognition on the organization website and social media

Position Descriptions

This section sets out the position descriptions for the management and volunteers, and the numbers needed.

Board of Directors (4-7)

The Chair & Champion's responsibilities include the following:

- Managing monthly board meetings
- Opening doors at government, nonprofits, and corporations
- Communicating in media and organizing the messages
- Managing organization governance and fiduciary responsibility
- Managing the organization strategic planning
- Hiring and managing management
- Authorizing organizational business plans and policies

VICE CHAIR OF BOARD

The Vice Chair takes the place of the Chair at board meetings and contributes to board activity including committee, board, and management activities.

SECRETARY AND DIRECTOR

The Secretary is responsible for board agendas, minutes, and organization documentation and records.

TREASURER AND DIRECTOR

The treasurer is responsible for oversight of financial transactions, reports, and policies.

DIRECTORs (2)

The director is responsible for contributing to board meetings, supporting the board executive committee and management, and interacting with committees and advisory boards.

All board member terms of office will be two years in a position and all will sign a confidentiality/noncompetition agreement.

Boards of Advisors

There will be boards of advisors of five members and a management representative who will meet for a maximum one hour monthly or bi-monthly conference call or videoconference meeting to discuss one or two agenda items.

ADVISOR

The advisor is responsible for bringing information, ideas, and suggestions to the advisory board meetings based on skills, knowledge, and experience. Also they need to provide connections where possible to support the organization and the TEAM.

Sample 12 — Continued

Committees

CHAIR/VICE CHAIR

The committee Chair is responsible for facilitating strategic and tactical planning and execution based on the organizational strategic and business plan approved by the board. The chair and members approve additional projects and tasks as identified.

COMMITTEE MEMBERS (4)

Committee members are responsible for specific committee assignments which may include projects and tasks done in the area of responsibility or in collaboration with members of other committees. One will be a back-up to the Chair.

COMMITTEE PROJECT MANAGERS (2) AND TASK ASSOCIATES (8)

These members will perform projects and tasks but will not need to meet with the functional committee, and will be able to work from home or office by phone or email.

AMBASSADOR

The ambassador will have a geographic territory and be responsible for communicating the messages and information of the organization via fliers/efliers, presentations to academic institutions, corporations, social enterprises, foundations, business groups, maker spaces, and other organizations using templates provided by the organization.

As appropriate, certain leads will be forwarded to the head office for a more detailed follow-up and discussion.

MENTORS/COACHES

Generalists and specialists may be recruited to support individuals and teams

e.g., http://www.socialmentornetwork.ca/

TERMS OF REFERENCE: COMMUNICATIONS, MARKETING, SALES, PARTNER/ALLIANCE COLLABORATIONS AND MEDIA COMMITTEE

Committee Overview:

The committee members will reflect members of the community and/or have experience and/or interest in communications, marketing, promotion, sales, partner/alliance collaboration, media, and volunteer management.

The committee will represent members from different areas: urban, rural.

Membership terms are two years, and can be renewed for one term —

Committee members will be expected to make best efforts to attend all committee meetings (min. 75%) and participate in at least one annual initiative.

The Chair and Vice Chair of the committee will be approved by the Board of Directors.

Purpose:

The primary purpose of this committee is to work with the board, management, advisory boards and other committees to build the brand name and messages direct and through media, reach different target audiences, generate revenue streams, create challenges and events and connect social innovators through partnerships and alliances, sponsorships, foundations, government support etc.

Key Objectives

- Contribute content to the annual and evolving strategic and business plan
- Define the price ranges for services, events and products to achieve revenue streams to support regular and special operating expenses

- Implement marketing approaches, events and social media to support the revenue generation streams of reaching various target market users and contributors
- Build local, regional and national partnerships with corporations, nonprofits, academic institutions, social enterprises, government offices, etc.
- Identify and evaluate potential new revenue sources, and as feasible, implement with the support of committee members, project members, member task associates, and with members of other committees and other partners/affiliates
- Contribute process, policy and procedures to the organization manual

Knowledge/Skills/Experience (or interest in learning)

- Some academic training or professional experience in volunteer and/or communication, marketing, promotion, social media
- Experience in a volunteer role/capacity and within a nonprofit organization
- Excellent communication skills verbally and in writing
- Good technology skills, analytical skills, and interviewing skills
- Self-motivated, independent, and can work well in a group environment

Time Commitment

Initially, the tasks outlined above will require considerable time until a team is recruited to perform sub tasks helping the champions. Most of this work can be performed by telephone, email, video conferencing etc., as decided by the team.

Once the core teams are recruited, the individual area plans established, training and manuals are completed, the ongoing time requirement will significantly decline, with emphasis on retention and recognition of volunteers, as well as defining new roles for the organization.

Benefits

- Learning and applying new skills, new methods and approaches in volunteer management
- Networking with a wide variety of individuals across the country
- Recognition by the organization by way of a letter to a supervisor or a letter outlining contributions to be included in a career portfolio and resume, or a testimonial to the business
- Recognition on the organization website and social media

TERMS OF REFERENCE — FINANCE COMMITTEE

Committee Overview:

The committee members will reflect members of the community and/or have experience and/or interest in financial management, accounting, bookkeeping, or banking.

The committee will represent members from across the country, and different areas: urban, rural.

Membership terms are two years, and can be renewed for one terms

Committee members will be expected to make best efforts to attend all committee meetings (min. 75%) and participate in at least one annual initiative.

The Chair of the committee will be approved by the Board of Directors.

Purpose:

The primary purpose of this committee is to establish the financial, accounting, bookkeeping processes, and tools, as well as support the financial sourcing and reporting in collaboration with other committees to report effectively to the board and advisory boards.

Sample 12 — Continued

Key Objectives

- Develop and revise financial statement projections
- Develop and implement financial transaction processing procedures
- Monitor actual financial results and produce monthly variance reports
- Develop and implement financial sourcing techniques with other committees (sponsorship, foundation and government grants, community bond, social investment, crowdfunding, services and product sales, challenge events, presentations/panels/gala/show/conference events, memberships, training, webinars, guides
- Develop transaction and report data for review and analysis of annual audit and transaction reporting
- Establish banking services and credit cards
- Develop process, forms, policy, and procedures for the organization manual

Knowledge/Skills/Experience (or interest in learning)

- Some academic training or professional experience in volunteer and/or bookkeeping, accounting or finance or administration management
- Experience in a volunteer role/capacity and within a nonprofit organization
- Excellent communication skills verbally and in writing
- Good technology skills, analytical skills, and interviewing skills
- Self-motivated, independent, and can work well in a group environment

Time Commitment

Initially, the tasks outlined above will require considerable time until a team is recruited to perform sub tasks helping the champions. Most of this work can be performed by telephone, email, videoconferencing etc., as decided by the team.

Once the core teams are recruited, the individual area plans established, training, and manuals are completed, the ongoing time requirement will significantly decline, with emphasis on retention and recognition of volunteers, as well as defining new roles for the organization.

Benefits

- Learning and applying new skills, new methods and approaches in volunteer management
- Networking with a wide variety of individuals across the country
- Recognition by the organization by way of a letter to a supervisor or a letter outlining contributions to be included in a career portfolio and resume, or a testimonial to the business
- Recognition on the organization website and social media

TERMS OF REFERENCE – TECHNOLOGY COMMITTEE

Committee Overview:

The committee members will reflect members of the community and/or have experience and/or interest in telephone and computer technology.

The committee will represent members from across the country, and different areas: urban, rural.

Membership terms are two years, and can be renewed for one terms

Committee members will be expected to make best efforts to attend all committee meetings (min. 75%) and participate in at least one annual initiative.

The Chair of the committee will be approved by the Board of Directors.

Sample 12 — Continued

Purpose:

The primary purpose of this committee is to establish the telephone and computer equipment and software to support the operations of the organization and its board, committees, and members.

Key Objectives

- Identify and acquire hardware and software telecommunication and computer equipment and software and tools to support organization requirements for operations, training, communication, marketing, conferencing, graphic design, sales credit card processing, bookkeeping, reporting, database information, etc.
- Design tools and procedures for use of hardware and software for other committees to support productivity and efficiency
- Upgrade tools and training to ensure effectiveness
- Contribute processes, procedures, policies to the organization manual.

Knowledge/Skills/Experience (or interest in learning)

- Some academic training or professional experience in volunteer and telecommunications/ computer hardware and software areas
- Experience in a volunteer role/capacity and within a nonprofit organization
- Excellent communication skills verbally and online and in writing
- Good technology skills, analytical skills, and interviewing skills
- Self-motivated, independent and can work well in a group environment

Time Commitment

Initially, the tasks outlined above will require considerable time until a team is recruited to perform sub tasks helping the champions. Most of this work can be performed by telephone, email, videoconferencing etc., as decided by the team.

Once the core teams are recruited, the individual area plans established, training, and manuals are completed, the ongoing time requirement will significantly decline, with emphasis on retention and recognition of volunteers, as well as defining new roles for the organization.

Benefits

- Learning and applying new skills, new methods and approaches in volunteer management
- Networking with a wide variety of individuals across the country
- Recognition by the organization by way of a letter to a supervisor or a letter outlining contributions to be included in a career portfolio and resume, or a testimonial to the business
- Recognition on the organization website and social media

TERMS OF REFERENCE – OPERATIONS & ADMINISTRATION COMMITTEE

Committee Overview:

The committee members will reflect members of the community and/or have experience and/or interest in operations and administration.

The committee will represent members from across the country, and different areas: urban, rural.

Membership terms are two years, and can be renewed for one terms

Committee members will be expected to make best efforts to attend all committee meetings (min. 75%) and participate in at least one annual initiative.

The Chair of the committee will be approved by the Board of Directors.

Sample 12 — Continued

Purpose:

The primary purpose of this committee is to establish and support the daily operations and administration of the organization as performed by the management team.

Key Objectives

- Manage daily operations
- Update online records
- File paper records
- Report non-standard requests to the board or committees or management on a priority basis
- Contribute processes, policies, and procedures to the organization manual.

Knowledge/Skills/Experience (or interest in learning)

- Some academic training or professional experience in volunteer and operations and administration
- Experience in a volunteer role/capacity and within a nonprofit organization
- Excellent communication skills verbally and in writing
- Good technology skills, analytical skills, and interviewing skills
- Self-motivated, independent, and can work well in a group environment

Time Commitment

Initially, the tasks outlined above will require considerable time until a team is recruited to perform sub tasks helping the champions. Most of this work can be performed by telephone, email, videoconferencing, etc., as decided by the team.

Once the core teams are recruited, the individual area plans established, training, and manuals are completed, the ongoing time requirement will significantly decline, with emphasis on retention and recognition of volunteers, as well as defining new roles for the organization.

Benefits

- Learning and applying new skills, new methods, and approaches in volunteer management
- Networking with a wide variety of individuals across the country
- Recognition by the organization by way of a letter to a supervisor or a letter outlining contributions to be included in a career portfolio and resume, or a testimonial to the business
- Recognition on the organization website and social media

Committee Members (4)

Members participate in quarterly committee meetings and take on specific assignments to support growth of the structure of the organization. Members may be assisted by project managers and task member associates in this committee and other committees.

Project Managers (2) and Task Committee Associates (20)

These members do NOT attend meetings, but support committee members on assignments which can generally be completed by phone, email, videoconferencing. The projects and tasks are performed when available to participate.

ensure that there are sufficient staff and volunteers to make the necessary difference.

- **Administration**: This committee supports the day-to-day administration, operations, technology and legal aspects of the enterprise. These are the critical pieces that allow everyone to make the difference. Part of their mandate is to ensure effective processes at the least possible cost.

- **Research and development**: This committee should actively search for alliances as well as investigate future opportunities in products, services, programs, and events. There may also be research done in support of the cause and for future communication. Often in the nonprofit space these publications would be shared with similar or related organizations.

3.6 Ambassadors and community teams

Having people passionate about the cause is the most important thing. Sometimes society doesn't openly recognize that the cause exists or it doesn't understand the full negative impact that is currently in existence. Having people actively promoting the cause is hugely beneficial to growing an organization's momentum.

Ambassadors are those individuals who are passionate about the cause and encourage others to be part of the movement. Community teams are clusters of these ambassadors working together.

Ambassadors are like patrons, but they are typically more motivated and involved as individuals in the work of the organization. Often, they have been impacted firsthand, have a loved one impacted, or have seen the impact and have been affected. So they are more than willing to promote the organization through presentations, word of mouth, social media, emails or letters, videos, and their personal stories, participation at events, interviews, or writing blogs or articles.

Having these individuals become part of your movement by providing an action for them or by communicating with them will help to build the network and awareness. The organization most likely wants to email or mail these people information directly and collect information on them and how to better support them. They have the responsibility in a geographic service area for communicating messages, recruiting volunteers, and identifying other supporters.

A single ambassador is worth more than a volunteer, as they'll probably bring in more volunteers. Treat them well and have a strategy to communicate with them.

Kickstarter

Kickstarter.com is a platform that allows organizations to be supported by the community. Sometimes an organization presells their products through the platform. Sometimes there are bonus gifts for giving to the organization early. An author might pledge to name a character in the book after someone who donates more than $1,000 to the initiative. Social initiatives that use this platform could provide special thank-yous for early support.

The community that invests in the social initiatives on Kickstarter get very engaged, and should be a way to recruit and connect with some of the first ambassadors.

As the number of ambassadors increases, there is an opportunity to connect them with each other. This is the emergence of Community teams.

Community teams are stronger than ambassadors as they work together and support each other in their work. Having a strategy to tie these individuals together is the next step.

Earth Rangers

Earth Rangers is a nonprofit organization that raises funds to support endangered animals and habitats. They work with schools to do animal shows and information sessions. At these sessions, students that are passionate about the environment are easily identified and encouraged to join the online community of Earth Rangers. The online platform encourages the youth to communicate the importance of the Earth Rangers campaign with their networks and raise funds. These youth are given additional information and online access to each other, creating a powerful network of ambassadors.

3.7 Peers

The peers within the sector have a lot to offer. Unlike other sectors, the social sector is extremely collaborative and open to sharing learnings with each other.

Learning from others who have already traveled your path can be extremely enlightening. Finding a networking group that gathers or simply attending sector events is helpful in learning and making these connections.

Ideally, a group of five or more organizations' leadership could meet monthly for about 30 minutes to share information, ideas, problems, and opportunities in a free-flowing discussion format.

3.8 Mentors and/or coaches

Having a mentor or coach during the start-up phase is helpful in keeping the executive director on track and being accountable to short-term goals that are created. The first few months can be quite emotional with great wins but a lot of setbacks. Having someone that the executive director can speak to about both emotional and organizational concerns can be extremely helpful.

As the organization grows, it is beneficial to have a leadership coach to help the executive director and management in growing their skill sets and managing the growing staff and volunteers.

3.9 Paid advisors

Being frugal and lean during the start-up stage is important, although there are some paid advisors that might be needed. For example, setting up the organization and incorporating it often benefits from a professional lawyer, accountant, insurance agent, technology person (website and social media), and banker.

As the organization grows, so will the need for specialized advice, such as the following:

- **Auditing:** In the first few years, the financials don't necessarily have to be audited but that changes as the operating budget increases and there are more stakeholders to report to.

- **Legal support:** Having a law firm that intimately understands your organization is helpful. If a problem arises, you want to minimize how long it takes to ramp up your legal advisor on the basics of the organization. As the organization grows, so will legal concerns. It becomes more financially beneficial to have a lawyer on retainer once a critical mass has been met.

- **Bookkeeping:** Keeping up-to-date records, especially with the number of transactions, quickly becomes something that could be outsourced.

- **Technology and security:** Technology in a growing organization quickly becomes more complicated and time consuming for the team. Luckily with technological advances there are affordable solutions for service providers.

Insurance and banking specialists are also beneficial to have on your side. Although these services are not in addition to the banking fees and insurance premiums, building a relationship with these individuals is helpful in the long run.

The key is that the number of people in the organization needs to be balanced with the financial sustainability of the organization. If there are a growing number of volunteers, there needs to be the management to support this in training and communications.

Define who you need to develop the social innovation and develop brief position descriptions of your core team.

Once you have a plan of who is needed, the recruitment of these people is next.

4. Recruitment

Now that the organization realizes who it needs to have on board to be successful, it must find these people.

4.1 The job description

In the social sector, the job description is much more than just a job description. It is a marketing tool.

It can't be assumed that everyone wants to work for your organization. Although the cause is great and there are good opportunities, the first thing to do is create a job posting that makes this apparent. In recruitment, you need to market the position just as much as the candidates need to market themselves. In fact, for volunteer roles, your ability to market the position is even more important.

How do you create this messaging? Think like the participants. Why would they wish to volunteer or work with your organization? It is often because they are able to realize benefits that are more than just the monetary benefits. For employees, the average position in nonprofit is paid less than the average position in for-profit, so there needs to be other reasons why people elect to work in the sector. For volunteers, this is even more apparent.

Participants must be provided with a clear list of measurable benefits. The job description should include:

- **Cause information:** What is the cause all about? What is the negative impact that is happening? How many people are being impacted? The importance of the cause needs to be illustrated clearly.

- **Organizational information:** How is the organization addressing the problem? Is there something that is unique about the organization and what are the positive impacts that have already been created?

- **Time commitment:** How much time is needed? Is this a contract, full-time, part-time, or volunteer position?

- **Benefits:** Include the list of benefits (beyond monetary).

4.2 Recruiting the core group

How do you reach people that might want to work or volunteer for your organization?

You need to start with a core group of supporters. This will get the momentum started. Informally ask family, friends, and associates if they would like to meet to discuss a social innovation idea and use an informal agenda to discuss a problem and parties impacted, and some areas of possible solutions. This could include the use of a mind-mapping exercise and a problem-solving approach.

Action: Talk informally about a problem, and who is impacted, with family, friends, and associates and ask if they would like to meet to discuss.

The social innovation starts with an individual or small team with an idea to solve a problem that has been identified. This leads to the formation of a core group who want to explore the viability of the solution or solutions ideas through research and feasibility analysis, including validation that the solutions meet the needs of the impacted parties, and that someone is willing to pay, subsidize, sponsor, or fund.

> **Action:** Core team begins to define the structure of the enterprise and recruit others to develop mini position descriptions and determine places to post for recruitment. Training, retention, and recognition must be planned.

Assuming a positive outcome, the next step will be the building of an infrastructure to further develop and plan the organization. In some circumstances this may require the recruitment and hiring, on a part-time basis, of a virtual assistant and a volunteer management coordinator. In most cases you will be seeking volunteers who have skills, knowledge, experience, or want to develop competencies to support their jobs/careers or desire to learn and apply.

4.3 External recruitment

Who else do you need? With the core group in place you are now able to do a broader recruitment strategy. With the job descriptions ready to be posted, it is time to research several sources where you can post volunteer and contract jobs. Part of this research is to read and understand the terms and conditions, and the fees if required.

Some places to research include:

- Volunteer centers
- Corporate CSR and in-kind
- Academic institutions
- Small-business centers
- Start-up weekends (immersing yourself in it for a weekend)
- Social innovation challenges
- MakerSpace which is a space where people can build things with the tools that are there (spaces.makerspace.com)
- Boards of Trade/Chambers of Commerce, business improvement associations

- Other business associations

- Charities and not-for-profits

    Action: Research individuals and organizations who can assist with recruitment of the team.

As recruitment is a part of marketing, consider using unique ways to attract volunteers or employees. One example is a postcard or eflier.

Remember to keep a database of contacts that you have used for recruitment including connected individuals, academic institutions, incubators/accelerators, business groups and clubs/organizations, volunteer centers, and patrons. This will help you in the future as you continue to recruit and grow.

As revenue grows, additional part-time resources may be defined, recruited, and trained to meet growth needs.

5. Training

Training involves orientation training for those who are onboard, and then ongoing training to advance the knowledge and skills of team members. Both are critical.

5.1 Orientation training

Orientation training ensures that new volunteers and employees are productive as quickly as possible. It has also been demonstrated that good orientation improves the chance that people will be retained as they have a positive first impression. Depending on the different roles, the orientation training could be quick and on the job, or it could involve intense off-site work and job shadowing.

All contract employees and volunteers must be provided with orientation training. Sample 13 includes excerpts from the whole operations guide which includes policies, processes, procedures, and forms, such as:

- Soft skills includes leadership, communication, and working with others in a team. It is all of the interpersonal skills that are needed for success in a social initiative.

Sample 13
Orientation Training

The Training step outlines the forms of training needed for all levels of the social enterprise and must include technical and soft skills, as well as product, program, consulting, and event skills where the trainee may not have skills, knowledge, and experience, or have some of the above but need to apply at higher levels.

ALL participants in the social enterprise must participate in an initial orientation training program that will include information, understanding of roles and responsibilities, support tools and resources, and application of specific skills.

An example training agenda is set out below:

1. Welcome and introductions
2. First steps: position description, guide and NDA, review of website
3. Project management and project lists
4. Monthly reporting
5. Bimonthly connecting
6. HQ support
7. Q&A

- Technical skills is all of the specific expertise needed for functional areas, specific technologies, or other specific skills.

- Cross-committee sessions is to have an understanding of projects, programs, and events that require members from one or more committees or input.

5.2 Ongoing training

Ongoing training is important not only for continuous development of the staff and volunteers, but it also helps them with their own professional development goals. By providing a budget for this, the organization can benefit from the improved skill set of the individual, but it also helps with retention as the individual is treated well and will appreciate this perk.

Ongoing training should be specific, based on both the needs of the organization as well as the needs of the individual. There often are annual discussions between the manager and the individual to craft the professional development goals for the year and the budget can be allocated for this.

5.3 Training methods

With technology and new training mechanisms available, there are more opportunities for good training to be made available to the organization at a reasonable cost:

- **In-person training**: Face-to-face training is critical when the subject is intensive and requires hands-on learning and interaction.

- **One-on-one coaching**: Ongoing support through coaching is beneficial for more complex, interpersonal skill development.

- **Online training and webinars**: This allows for access to experts around the world, training based on the individual's ability, and often is available at a lower price point. Webinars are often smaller chunks of content that can be available from a wide variety of speakers. The topics can be very niche and also involve participant interaction.

- **Conferences**: Conferences can have a variety of topics that can be selected based on the individual's interest. The added benefits are the networking opportunities and the quality of the speakers (often quite high). Participants can bring information back to the organization and provide in-person and written summaries of learnings that could be applied.

6. Retention

Retention involves strategies to communicate to motivate people to continue to be part of the team.

Management, the board, advisors, and committees must develop and apply a variety of techniques to retain employees and volunteers to ensure organizational sustainability. Some tactics include:

- Reinforcing the benefits.

- Regular communication that provides updates and stories of success.

- Regular involvement in decision making and making sure voices are being heard.

- Interaction with each other.

- Ongoing training and skills updates.

- Cross-committee sessions includes the ongoing communication of different parties to ensure that all voices are heard.

- Increasing responsibility or remuneration.

- Recognition! This is one of the most understated of them all.

Any way to build community and connection between people involved in the cause will help with retention. We are going to spend a bit more time on recognition, based on its importance.

7. Recognition

Recognition is all about showing people that they make a difference not only as team members, but to those impacted by the contributions they make.

All employees and volunteers must be recognized for their contributions to the organization in several different ways. This can be in person or in written form, or by way of a small gift or an award, or a thank-you. Some specific examples include:

- Letter from the chair of the board or executive director.

- Certificate of achievement or time committed.

- Pin, ribbon, medal, or other physical thank you.

- Mug, hat, T-shirt, or other promotional products

- Recognition at events through award ceremony or the name on the program

- Website and social media recognition of the person's work. One way is not enough. Recognition uses a variety of tools and techniques to support the contributions of the people involved. The more forms and methods used the better it will be for the team.

CHAPTER 6
HOW THE ORGANIZATION WORKS

All the strategy is now in place and you are ready for takeoff. It is the operations and the how the organization will work that becomes top of mind. Some immediate questions when thinking about practicality are:

- How will the organization be structured?

- What does the day-to-day look like?

How the organization operates includes some of these backbone functions:

- **Start-up tasks:** These are activities that happen one time. These activities will lay the foundation that the organization needs to grow upon.

- **Day-to-day activities:** The day-to-day tasks that are necessary to the ongoing operations of the organization.

- **Technology:** Technology is a basic requirement of business. For social initiatives, technology can be used to grow even faster and to make more of a social impact.

- **Periodic tasks:** Specific tasks that happen once a month or a year including the legal and accounting requirements.

1. Start-up Tasks

The first few weeks and months of launching an organization always start with a flurry. There is a need to do a combination of necessary pieces and also strategic pieces. The first few months is always a struggle of prioritizing what to do. Like most large projects and difficult tasks, the best thing is to put your nose to the grindstone and start getting these tasks listed, put start and end dates, a cost if necessary, and who is responsible.

Here is a quick list of things to consider and a potential prioritization list to get started.

1.1 Step 1: Space needs assessment

Are you going to be a virtual organization with everyone working from their homes or are you going to have space? Do you need dedicated space or could an incubator or coworking space work? Is there a need for storage of files or products?

Identify what office and storage space is required for your organization. What is the square footage for regular activities with furniture and equipment? Do you need a boardroom? Just office space? An area to collaborate and brainstorm? What would be optimal for the organization? Don't forget square footage for storage space for items such as filing cabinets and boxes.

Space is one of the most costly parts of starting up an organization. Although it is great to think big and have a list of space requirements that you'd like to have, it is also important to understand which of these criteria are nice-to-haves versus need-to-haves.

1.2 Step 2: Find space

Is space even necessary? Determine whether space is even needed or if there are other ways to operate for the first few months or even year. For example, there are many coworking spaces and hubs for social entrepreneurs to have space when needed. Even hugely successful organizations such as Microsoft started in a garage.

Space could simply be your own home office or garage. Is it possible to do most of your work at home? By doing this you not only save on the cost of real estate to rent or buy, but you can do tax write-offs for using the space (check with your accountant).

You might require an office location. This is likely if you are starting with multiple workers or volunteers, or if it is anticipated that you will be expanding rapidly. This is also needed if a large percentage of the work needs more space or different space than you have available at your home. Some people decide to rent space knowing that they will be more effective working outside of their homes.

Another alternative is sharing space in a coworking space. This can allow you to rent the boardrooms or meetings rooms when required. You can also have access to desks for the days of the week or times when working from home doesn't make sense, which are called "hot desks."

Social Impact Hubs

Social Impact Hubs are found throughout North America and often in major urban centers. They provide coworking space and additional amenities including Internet, printing, and administration. These hubs also provide community and professional development opportunities.

Initially you will probably operate from a home office environment unless space or a coworking space is available free or at a low cost. If signing a lease, make sure that you engage with a lawyer and be careful regarding the terms and conditions.

1.3 Step 3: Equipment

The initial costs beyond space can be quite extensive with the need to have all of the furniture and equipment up and running. This can include:

- Desk(s)
- Chair(s)
- Table(s)

- Couch(es)

- Lighting

- Filing cabinet(s)

- Technology requirements including a computer, printer, and server

Often the first reflex is to purchase equipment. As a social initiative, the more money that you save up front, the more social impact can be made. Do you need to buy everything?

Could you have some of the items donated? Older computers are a little trickier due to their shorter lifespans and the ever-changing technology, but filing cabinets and office equipment is often made available when a for-profit organization downsizes or moves its office space. Organizations such as Habitat for Humanity Restores can provide furniture and equipment at 40 percent or more off of retail costs.

Another alternative is to lease equipment, which is a common way to purchase large pieces of equipment (most notably photocopiers). Ensure that if you are signing a lease, that you understand the duration of the lease and acknowledge that this adds to your ongoing costs of being in business. Also, if the organization doesn't get off the ground, these leases are a liability that need to be considered and have to be paid out.

1.4 Step 4: Monthly expenses

The ongoing utilities and monthly expenses of running an organization need to be considered. Just like in a new home, the office needs to have some of these basic amenities:

- **Electricity and water:** If you are in a home office, these are absorbed into your normal costs but recognize that the electricity bill might be higher with someone being in the home all day. In a new office space or coworking space, this cost would be part of the monthly rent.

- **Telephone:** This could be a landline or you might be able to use your cell phone. As the organization grows, there might be a more complicated telecommunications system or even a 1-800 number to be set up. In a new office space, this would need to be set up. In a coworking space, you would most likely rely on your cell phone or set up a VoIP calling system such as Skype, FaceTime, or Google Hangouts.

- **Internet:** In a home office, this is most likely already in place. However the usage would increase. In a new office space, this would have to be set up. In a coworking space, this would be included.

Be careful to minimize these monthly expenses. These ongoing expenses increase the overall budget of the organization tremendously. The more that you can limit these, the lower your break-even is.

Note: Break-even is the amount of income that your organization must make to make zero ($0) profit. Break-even will be further discussed in the next chapter.

1.5 Step 5: Organization registration

Now is the time to register the social enterprise. This will be as either a nonprofit, as a for-profit, or as a charity, and later may be a B Corp.

- **Nonprofit:** This organization is not permitted to make a significant profit, it must have a board of directors, and there is no ownership by an individual. There are tax benefits to this structure and there are other controls in place.

- **For-profit:** This organization has the least amount of control by the government, but is required to pay taxes. A for-profit can be set up as either a sole proprietorship, partnership, or corporation. The terminology, advantages, and disadvantages will vary by country and governments that are in place.

- **Charity:** This organization can receive donations and issue tax receipts. They can transfer funds to other charities. This structure has more controls in place by the government and must follow these stricter rules to maintain charitable status.

Another emerging organizational type is popping up in some states and provinces: one name it goes by is the Community Interest Corporation. This is where an organization is technically a for-profit but is given preferential treatment by the government based on a portion of the profits pledged to be put to community good. Once an organization has been set up in this way, it is impossible for the profits to revert back to the owners and to retract this pledge. A new organization would have to be set up in order to do this.

It takes very little time to do the actual paperwork to set up the organization. The difficult part is in deciding which structure makes the most sense. Often the board of directors discusses the official structure, there might be some legal consultation in advance, and often there is a lot of additional research.

Another opportunity is to register your organization as a B Corp. B Corps are a new type of business that uses the power of business that follows specific policies and ways of being socially and environmentally responsible. No matter what the legal structure is of the organization, this is a registration that is more of a marketing and operational guideline. Registering as a B Corp can be more time consuming with many processes and operational changes necessary. There is also the rigor of the B Corp certification organization that does its due diligence and requires ongoing documentation to validate your organization's continuing B Corp status.

Regardless of the decisions that are made here, it is important to note that they are difficult to undo. Doing the work upfront is paramount.

1.6 Step 6: Banking

Once an organization has been registered, it is possible for it to have a bank account. In fact, often multiple accounts are opened to help manage the budget of various facets of the organization.

An account could be opened with either a bank, trust, or credit union. Check the fees for deposits, checks, use of ATM and online tools, credit card rate, operating, and term loan rates.

Make sure the person opening the account has a good credit rating from either Equifax or TransUnion as banks can sometimes reject applications based on the result.

1.7 Step 7: Marketing basics

These are the marketing pieces that help in establishing that the organization is a going concern. Here are some standard pieces to consider:

- Business cards with the name of the organization, logo, and a tagline
- Letterhead
- Website

- Social media accounts

Don't overprint at the beginning. Get a small amount of business cards and letterhead to allow flexibility if things change in the first six months.

If you aren't sure where to begin designing these items, there are templates available from most online printing companies. Two of the most commonly used ones are Vistaprint and Staples.

1.8 Step 8: Selecting paid advisors

Throughout the start-up of the organization there will be specific professional service providers that it will be good to access. There is a Paid Advisory Team tracking sheet on the download kit for you to use as you do your research.

- **Banker:** Not only is your bank account important to set up, but starting to build a relationship with the banker individually is also helpful. If you end up needing a line of credit or a loan in the future, it is always easier to start the process when a relationship is already formed. In addition, the banker might have local connections in the community to help you. The more he or she knows about what you are up to, the more beneficial and potential connections that could be made.

- **Bookkeeper/accountant:** A bookkeeper or an accountant is an individual to keep track of your accounts. This helps with your financial planning and decision making as the organization grows. It is important to have one early on.

- **Paralegal/lawyer:** Protecting your organization against risk is this professional's role. Paralegals have more limitations in the legal support they can provide but they are more affordable. A lawyer is more expensive, but more extensive in the coverage he or she is able to provide.

- **Insurance agent:** Insurance can be purchased for almost anything. Understanding the risks that you are bearing and how to protect yourself against this is where the insurance agent is helpful.

- **Administrative assistant:** There are a lot of moving parts and a lot of work to do! Having an administrative assistant (either in person or a virtual assistant), can help your organization scale up faster by helping you with the tactical tasks and the image of the organization.

Action: Individually or with your core team complete the tasks and others that you identify within a specific timeline and budget.

2. Day-to-Day Activities

Running a socially focused organization involves a lot of moving parts. There are day-to-day activities (outside of the strategy and growth of the organization) that need to be attended to.

2.1 Governance

The board of directors should be integrated into the organization early on. This requires a regular schedule of meetings and communication mechanism to keep everyone engaged.

The meetings in the beginning should be more frequently scheduled as the board of directors is acting as an operational board. It is good to have meetings every two weeks; enough for tasks to be completed between meetings and still enough time to build momentum. Each meeting should have the following:

- **Agenda:** What will be discussed in the meeting? By having an agenda (and support documents), people can come prepared to the meeting which will make them more effective. It also helps with people's expectations of what to expect in the discussion.

- **Success measurements:** There may not be measurements that will be decided upon now, but there should be some measures that are looked at each meeting to help with impartially watching the momentum. Some examples of things to measure in the early stages could be the number of volunteers, the number of new clients, or the number of new connections that are made.

- **General updates:** What is happening? Giving an overall update for everyone to be on the same page is helpful. The update can include a list of achievements rather than be about discussion or making decisions.

- **Discussions:** Each meeting should have some time and a topic dedicated to open discussion. This allows for engagement and ownership of the decision-making process. It is good to only have one discussion topic at each meeting to minimize the length of the meeting and to allow everyone to stay focused.

- **Referrals:** A time specifically for the board of directors to bring to the forefront people or organizations that should be getting involved. This puts it on the agenda and keeps it top of mind. It is for the board to remember that its network is a key part of its role in the success of the organization.

- **Minutes:** Keeping track of what has occurred in meetings is helpful. It can update people who were missing. It can help in the future with annual reports and other messaging. It will also ensure that there is action based on the decisions that are made at these meetings.

Between meetings there should be regular updates and email discussions.

Eventually, the board meetings would change to once every month or even every quarter. Over time, the board of directors moves from an operational board to more governance and strategy.

2.2 Administration

The administrator keeps everything on track. He or she can perform general duties such as answering phone and email requests, calendaring, updating the database and bookkeeping records, banking, voucher records, and almost anything else that is needed. Typically the importance and impact of a great administrator is under-realized.

When hiring an administrator there are a few key traits that you should be looking for:

- **Organization:** With all of the various jobs and files to be handled, being able to keep everything straight is important.

- **Detailed:** A lot of the initial work will be surrounding remembering details, names, and ensuring that the "t's are crossed and i's are dotted."

- **Friendly:** Being willing and able to communicate with people over the phone and face-to-face is important.

- **Multitasker:** With the variety of tasks and demands of a small organization, it is important that he or she is able to move smoothly from one task to another and back again.

- **Flexible:** Every day will be different. This is the type of atmosphere that would suit someone comfortable with change.

Another attribute would be having strengths that are the opposite of the strengths of the president or executive director. They should complement each other.

3. Technology

Technology is no longer something an organization can avoid. In many instances, technology can still be leveraged to do more with less. In the nonprofit space, it can be a significant competitive advantage.

3.1 Telephone system

Often your telephone system is the first interaction with your organization. What does your telephone system say about you? See the download kit for tips when answering your telephone or email, and for your voicemail message.

In the start-up stage, it is common for the main phone number to go directly to the founder. However, quickly it becomes important to have a telephone system that accesses multiple contacts as well as being user friendly. Quality and affordable telephone and computer hardware and software should be in place to support the office team. As the volume of inquiries grows, it may be necessary to include the use of an answering service which would email you the contact and subject information for you to follow up such as Call Ruby or Answer Plus.

The best practice is to always pick up the phone. Many phone systems will actually reroute phone calls to cell phones and to different phones within the organization to ensure that anyone calling reaches a live person. The more that you can limit voicemail, the better. People don't call to leave a message!

If people do go to voicemail, what does your voicemail say about you? You want to control your branding even here. A voicemail should be informative, especially when it comes to finding more information (which is why the person called!). Ensure that it includes a reference to the website where more information might be found. Voicemails should have a response time that the organization commits to. Sooner is always better to show that the caller matters.

3.2 Email

Almost everyone uses email. Whoever creates your website will be able to set you up with a customized email. This is a best practice as it lends credibility to you and the organization as well as immediately indicating to people that you have a website with more information.

If you are not able to have an email with your website, you can also create your own email through one of the email hosting services such as Hotmail, Gmail, or Yahoo!.

Once you have an email set up, make sure to set up an email signature. This should include your address and phone number, as people will refer back to your email address to get in touch with you at later dates. Also consider including links to other information or other branding information. Some organizations change their email signatures regularly and people respond to this.

Another good practice to start with is to have a policy of response times for emails. Sometimes it is difficult not to respond to emails immediately, but for time management best practices it is best to respond to emails during a dedicated portion of the day.

3.2a In addition to email

Email is not the only way to communicate in writing. Consider some of the others that have a perception of being more responsive:

- **Live chat:** Could you add this function to your website? In many cases, a pop up window lets the website viewer know that this is an option. Especially for organizations that provide coaching or support, it is a good way to reach out proactively to people already interested in your work.

- **Twitter or social media:** Some organizations prefer to respond to all general and customer-related questions through social media. It requires someone to monitor the feeds, but social media feeds go directly to smartphones which allows us to be quite responsive. It has the added benefit that these messages to customers then answer multiple people's questions at the same time and also of being a marketing tool about the work that you are doing.

3.2b Calendars within email software

A major part of most email software is its interaction with calendars. Calendars can be shared with teams so everyone can see your schedule and find times for meetings. This works well within an organization or when there is a trusted relationship.

But there are new tools that allow people from different organizations to find meeting times. Some examples are Call Ruby or Answer Plus.

3.3 Software

Software that should be considered in the operations of the organization:

- **Operating software:** What is the core software that is on your computers? Historically this has been software that you download on your computer and have to upgrade periodically or when you purchase new hardware. Now there is a trend toward cloud operating software.

- **Customer Relationship Management (CRM):** How do you keep track of your contacts? How do you keep track of the relationships that you have? As a nonprofit or social enterprise, there are more types of people to keep track of as there are clients, employees, and suppliers like a for-profit. There are also volunteers, donors, partners, government, funders, and many more stakeholders to keep track of. A CRM is a technology tool that keeps tracks of names, contact information, and many other details to keep your organization informed. Some CRMs can also interact with email marketing tools to have both software pieces working together.

- **Knowledge management/databases:** How do you store information? The files, the learnings, the research, the reports, and any other documentation that your organization collects should be organized in a way for future learnings, easy access, and legal requirements. Some popular ways to do this include a private server, Dropbox, Sharepoint, or Google Drive.

- **Project management software:** Are there other software platforms that can make you more effective? If working on a large project, is there project management software that could be helpful? Are there forms or other databases that need to be created? Are there any processes that could be automated?

3.4 Website/online store

Websites are a mandatory part of businesses, charities, nonprofits, and social enterprises.

Websites can be simplistic or they can be quite complicated.

If you are starting out without a budget, there are free content management systems (CMS) available to get you started including Wordpress, or you can start with a blogging platform such as Blogger to build your content.

If you do have a budget, you can hire a website company to build your site. Often it is still best to have them use a known content management system so that your own organization or volunteers can easily keep it updated.

Some key elements that a nonprofit or social enterprise should have on the website:

- **Call to action:** Could you ask for someone to donate or volunteer on the website? This is your action! People coming to the website and learning about your work should be provided with something to do about it.

- **Stories:** Your organization is making a big difference out there. Tell that story! Often the best story is the reason why you decided to start doing this work to begin with. Video stories from those impacted can be posted on the website and on social media.

- **Testimonials:** Not only are you helping your clients, but your volunteers, staff, partners, and funders all have testimonials to share about working with you.

- **Contact information:** How else do they reach you? Contact information should always be easily accessible. Contact forms are not recommended as they add a barrier to being contacted and are less friendly.

Another option that might be beneficial for social enterprises is to consider including an eStore functionality within the website to sell your products or services. This can be done within the website itself, but it might be better to link into existing ecommerce sites such Etsy, eBay, Yahoo! Store, or Kijiji.

3.5 Payroll and bookkeeping

There are some main software items for payroll and bookkeeping that are affordable so you don't have to do it all on paper anymore. Some to take a look at are Wave Apps, Freshbooks, Sage Accounting, or Quick-Books.

A key consideration in your selection of this software is what is easy for your volunteer or bookkeeper to use on a regular basis. And does this software integrate with your accountant so that year-end accounting and tax analysis is quick and easy?

3.6 Security

For everything to do with technology, security is always a concern. With all of the hacks that have occurred, this is a reasonable concern for any organization. Is your information safe? As the organization grows, Sharepoint or another security tool must be purchased, installed, and maintained.

Is the information stored on site, on your hardware? If it is, you need to consider what happens if something occurs to your building including theft, fire, flooding, or some other disaster that threatens your data. Are there backups? And how are those protected?

Security rules are always important to understand and be intentional about. Most databases and knowledge management systems allow for detailed records of view and edit capabilities of files.

Many organizations will ask individuals with access to information to sign documentation regarding this secure information.

Beyond this basic security, are there other policies in place? Some organizations require people's computers and phones to time out after a few minutes so that a password is needed to access information. Are there specific policies in place to protect your information?

4. Periodic Tasks

A number of additional tasks will be required periodically such as planning and conducting regular monthly meetings, or some may be one-time only tasks such as a subject-specific stakeholder meeting conference/convention/trade show. It could involve making presentations to groups and organizations and creating and setting up a booth.

Presentations can be saved and customized to the group being addressed. Booth set-up and support materials can have a standard format and then be customized to the audience.

Other periodic tasks could be making banking arrangements, insurance arrangements, accounting and legal arrangements, and annual reporting for tax purposes. These should be reviewed, evaluated, and put on the calendar on an as-needed or annual basis to ensure quality and affordability, and state who should perform the task.

4.1 Banking

Regular monitoring of the bank accounts, the fees incurred, and meeting with the banker are recommended throughout the lifespan of any organization.

4.2 Insurance

Determine fire/flood/theft and liability requirements and then get at least two premium estimates before deciding. Once this is in place, insurance is reassessed close to the end of the contract.

Many insurance agents and brokers will not understand what a social enterprise is so some education will be needed in order to determine the forms of coverage and the premium costs. Do not rush your decision in this area. Get input from your board members, associates, and other organizations, and shop at least two organizations to compare coverage and premium details.

4.3 Accounting

A bookkeeper or accountant might only be needed periodically to set up a chart of accounts and then do interim reporting. The accountant can provide overall tax planning, management, and reporting.

A chart of accounts is based on what the assets, liabilities, and net worth sections are in the bookkeeping system that you are establishing. The software you select may include suggested charts or a bookkeeper may include this when he or she sets up your system of accounts.

4.4 Legal arrangements

Lawyers can be expensive. A best practice is to research samples of the legal documents that you need, create a draft that takes your context into account, and then hire a lawyer to review. Make sure you get an estimate or firm quotation before hiring.

Some areas where it might be beneficial to consider legal advice:

- Registering the business. Once you have decided the legal form that you would like your organization to take, it is then good to have the assistance of a lawyer, especially when setting up a corporation or a nonprofit. A sole proprietorship and partnership are the simplest forms of establishing the organization and can usually be registered online but have no name protection and unlimited liability.

- Registering a trade name.

- Lease agreements, when negotiating space or equipment acquisition.

- Contracts and licenses with suppliers, customers, and partners.

- Hiring a contractor or employee (although this could use human resource support instead).

Action: Review legal registration options and decide what form to legally start the organization based on both legal and accounting advice.

5. Operations Guide

An operations guide is helpful as your organization grows. It should support all areas of the enterprise and should be used as a reference to support new employees and volunteers. Basically it should be able to answer questions and might even be available on the website. See the Suggested Table of Contents for Your Operations, Technology and Administration Guide on the download kit included with this book.

The challenge is that the guide needs to be maintained and kept current as the correct information needs to be in there. This means it is updated quite regularly which can be time consuming, but the benefits of helping to get new team members up to date should be a good enough justification. A huge advantage is that team members will be able to more readily share their duties and be backups to support situations for vacation, illness, and turnover.

The guide should include processes, procedures, forms, and policies — pretty much everything about the organization! Each page needs to have the date of the creation or revision and the initials of the author. A quarterly review should be conducted to ensure that all parts of the guide are current; perhaps someone in the organization can own the living document.

CHAPTER 7
FINANCE IN THE SOCIAL SECTOR

When you think of finance, what do you think? Wall Street, big banks, huge investment companies, and the for-profit world? So when we enter the world of finance with a social slant, we turn the way that we look at finance upside down.

The concept of leveraging finance in the social sector has been around for a while. (Social finance has been around for decades.) Investing in infrastructure in emerging markets has been happening for more than 100 years and micro-lending programs were around shortly after. But with the change to the new economy, the need for an understanding of finance and its implications within the sector are changing.

Initially, finance might be seen as unimportant. And in many social organizations, nonexistent. A common thing to hear within the nonprofit sector is that the organization is "not a business."

Why is finance so important? Every nonprofit and social enterprise in the entire world needs money to operate. Just because the organization is called a nonprofit, doesn't mean that it doesn't make money. In fact, they all need to make money in order to pay operating costs and they should have a reserve fund to ensure sustainability in this age.

All of these concerns with money are magnified when considering that the number and amount of donations are declining in this age.

An emerging thought surrounding social enterprise is that they need to scale. Often nonprofits and social enterprises decide not to scale as they believe that scaling will put their existing efforts at risk. They would rather continue to help 200 people than attempt scaling and risking closure. They are concerned that they are financially stretching themselves which makes financial planning important.

Traditional funding options are hesitant to enter this field as they don't want to be connected with a social organization that is financially unstable. This puts the financial institution between a rock and a hard place, as they don't want to lose money, but they also don't want to be responsible for closing the social organization. Either way they lose, so many don't work with any nonprofits at all.

1. Nonprofits and Social Enterprises Are Businesses in Many Ways

Everyone needs to pay for their operations. Money is used to pay for the staff, rent, utilities, supplies, and any other expense that is incurred. The more money that an organization has, the more social benefit as it can hire more people and leverage more resources.

If an organization cannot pay for the staff, they are let go and are no longer able to do their work. If an organization cannot pay for supplies, it is less effective and not able to run programs. Making money is part of business, and making money is critical for every nonprofit and social enterprise to keep doing work.

There are some significant differences:

- Nonprofits and social enterprises have social missions that take precedence over profits.

- There are some significant tax breaks for nonprofits that reduce the overall operational expense.

In the end, money is the difference between sustainability and closure.

Social enterprises that rely on the sale of products or services compete directly with for-profit businesses. Although the precedent is the mission, there is an understanding that business best practices actually allow the organization to make more of an impact and ensure their sustainability. In fact, the more social initiatives that focus on being competitive versus their for-profit competitors, the stronger the sector will be.

Out of this World Café

Out of this World Café is a café based on the main floor of an addiction and mental health hospital. They hire past patients and provide delicious and healthy food. The manager of the organization understands that customers come to the café the first time to make a social difference. They return time and time again, as the café's focused on being head to head in quality and taste with a for-profit café.

Money can also help organizations to grow. It takes money to buy new equipment, purchase more assets, and hire more people. It is these actions that allow the organization to grow in scale and therefore help more people. When an organization is looking at themselves like a business, they are able to do their financial and strategic planning in a risk-mitigated way.

2. Making Profit in the Nonprofit World

Just like in a for-profit organization, the nonprofit and social enterprise list both their income and their costs in any financials. The difference is the subheadings.

Typically a for-profit would highlight some of the following income streams:

- Sales of products
- Sales of services
- Investment income

Whereas a nonprofit could have:

- Donations
- Sales of products
- Sales of services
- Investment income
- Fundraising
- Sponsorships
- Granting
- Membership fees

In the new economy, the nonprofit or social enterprise has the luxury of having both. This is the new path to sustainability.

2.1 Donations

Regular donations are the most traditional source of income for a nonprofit. Often the organizations focus on the smaller and regular donations (or gifts) and then there are the major or one-time gifts.

Although this is still a prime source of income, with the percentage of the population donating in decline and the average donation amount also in decline, the pool of regular donors is no longer what it used to be. This has the social sector seeking income elsewhere.

2.2 Fundraising events

Fundraising events can be fantastic! Some signature fundraising events can support the fundraising requirements of an organization for an entire year. The amount of work that goes into these large events can be overwhelming. Plus it is risky to have all of the funding for an organization to be reliant on a single event.

Still, the benefits of doing this well can be substantial as well as fostering camaraderie amongst the team that is running the event. Some event examples would be a silent auction, live auction, gala, music night, speaker series, other entertainment, a competition, or a conference.

The challenge is that these events can be quite time consuming and the benefits need to be weighed against the effort of other income streams.

2.3 Sponsorships

Sponsorship support for programs, events, webinars, workshops, or just the organization in general are possible. Most organizations have sponsorship as part of their marketing budget allotment. Sponsorships can come from all types of organizations from the government, nonprofits, for-profits, and foundations. This includes internal groups under the heading of corporate social responsibility supporting community.

The key is to be able to clearly identify and communicate the measurable benefits to the organization.

2.4 Granting

Granting is still a major type of income for an organization. Grants are available through a plethora of organizations such as foundations, government, and corporations. Depending on the subsector, granting can be quite significant with education and healthcare getting a large amount of their funding from these sources.

The challenge with grants is that there are often more conditions to this funding than a traditional loan and definitely more than with fundraising or donor dollars. Also, there is often some learning in terms of the requirements of the grantee prior to being given funding. This is due to a relationship being necessary and the grant application is not always clear about the underlying values of the organization.

Some key points about writing grant applications:

- **Meet with the organization:** If you haven't met with them or spoken with them, there is little chance of getting the grant. Just like any decision, even granting is based on emotion and relationship. Make sure that they understand your organization and that you understand theirs.

- **Adhere to the content requirements:** There is a reason why the questions are there! Don't miss out on answering the questions that they are the most interested in. In your conversation with them, you might even ask which questions are the most important.

- **Partnerships:** The more the merrier. Always list your partnerships. Showing that other organizations like to work with you and that you are open to collaboration is always to your advantage. Don't forget to gather the letters of support early.

- **Tell stories:** Stories bring the work that your organization is doing to life. Highlight those.

- **Be specific about outputs and outcomes:** What have you concretely accomplished? Talk about those and list numbers where appropriate. By saying that your organization has made a big impact is not as powerful a statement as saying that your organization has made a big impact in 500 people's lives.

- **Don't assume benefits are obvious:** If the effort connects to, or benefits other areas, point this out. Don't take it for granted and think the reader will make this connection themselves.

- **Timelines matter:** Be explicit about the timeline of the project. But give yourself time! Usually when planning the timelines you want to at least double them as the unexpected is bound to happen. Include milestones!

- **Include the team:** Be clear about who will do what jobs and who will have what responsibilities and accountability. Include the team's credentials, knowledge, experience, skills, project management experience, leadership skills, and past success.

- **Keep it simple:** Keep the proposal compact and use language that everyone can understand.

Now you have a great grant proposal.

2.5 Membership fees

Membership fees are commonly used income streams for nonprofit organizations. They are used by cooperatives, associations, and other groups. They can be subscriptions to services or program fees.

Membership fees are expanding to have more value-added services with them. Your organization may consider establishing a fee range of memberships from individual to group to corporate and based on different levels of participation and benefits.

2.6 Sale of product and services

Products and services are often provided through social initiatives and many times in different ways to disrupt the for-profit space. Estores for services and products and combo product/service packages where customers and clients can purchase online or schedule discussions for further information can be created. Possible contacts can be located anywhere. An estore link could be shown on other websites and on business cards and emails. Some other ways to make money include:

- Fees for presenting as a keynote speakers or demonstrator or as part of a panel through direct contact or signing up as a client of a speakers' bureau to community organizations, academic groups, conventions, conferences, businesses.

- Lunch 'n' learn presentations for organization, corporation, or government groups that may be 15-45 minutes and may be done in one or a group of sessions in person or by video conference.

- Fees for interviews or articles.

- Webinar and/or workshop series that could be live and/or recorded and packaged as a group of five sessions or more.

- Combinations of the above.

2.7 Investment

Investing in your own organization's future is another option. This is the concept of creating an investment property or an arm of the organization that is able to subsidize the other work. Is there an opportunity that the social organization can invest in that would result in long-term financial gain?

Often a social organization would prefer that this type of an ongoing investment would not only provide continuous income, but it would also make a social impact at the same time.

2.7a Investing in a renewable energy project

Investing in renewable energy is a popular investment for social organizations, especially over the last two decades as many governments provide subsidies that make these investments both guaranteed as well as financially rewarding. Some states and provinces have elected to subsidize this industry more heavily than others including both

California and Ontario, and the result has been a surge in renewable energy sources.

Solar panels have been leveraged by for-profit organizations, but the nonprofit sector has also explored this area. You will often find camps that are energy self-sufficient or churches that have put solar panels on their roofs. Having a financial investment that also supports an organization's values makes this a great fit.

Indigenous Community

An indigenous community was hoping to provide economic development opportunities for the community while enabling the community to become energy self-sustaining. The solution was to invest in a wind turbine which would generate enough power to not only sustain the community but also allow for a large portion to be sold back into the power grid. The workers hired were from the community itself, which created employment opportunities as well as on-the-job training for the members of the community to be eligible for future wind turbine projects and sustainable employment. The end result is a community with more skilled labor, a reduction in the cost of energy for everyone, and an ongoing income stream.

2.7b Investing in property

Real estate is another investment that can be leveraged for both income and mission. Historically the value of real estate has increased. In Europe it is common for people to own their homes if they inherited them, and the same trend is beginning in North America. With this understanding of the value of the real estate market, many of the larger nonprofits have legacy land assets which they can leverage. Legions, Rotary and Lions Clubs, Salvation Army, and many faith organizations have real estate that can be used for good as well as a financial return.

Long-Term Care Facility

A church had excess land which it felt could be used for community needs. They investigated what type of housing was needed in the community and identified that there was a rise in seniors and they were being forced out of the neighborhood once they were no longer self-sufficient.

The church partnered with a developer and a long-term care organization to build a long-term care facility on adjoining property. Not only were the seniors no longer forced out of the community, but the church could support them even further through social activities and programming.

In addition, the church retained a percentage of the ownership of the long-term care facility, receiving their profit share on an annual basis.

Even the smaller and newer nonprofits and social enterprises can consider real estate and property opportunities. Sometimes a nonprofit is gifted property and understands not just the current value, but the future or potential value.

Building Up

Building Up is a social enterprise that trains marginalized youth in trades. A foundation offered to loan them $1 million dollars if it could turn around and invest that funding. It decided to purchase a piece of real estate that required renovation work. This was a win-win as the project allowed it to teach the youth variety in trades from plumbing to drywalling and it was able to retain the building after fixing it up.

2.7c Business type ideas

Beyond a renewable energy project or investing in real estate, there are other business-type ideas that a social organization might consider. The key is to ensure that they have there two components:

- **Asset based:** There should be something that is being invested in that is typically tangible. For renewable energy, it is in the equipment, be it the solar panels or the wind turbine. For real estate, it is the land or building. For other options, it could be equipment such as a stove or a truck; having something that has value.

- **Financial return:** The idea needs to have a financial return. The lower the risk the better. For renewable energy there are fixed contracts with the government of how much they will buy the energy for and for what time period, the return is known upfront and it is virtually no-risk as the contract is with the government.

For real estate, the return is not known and not as guaranteed, but this could also mean that the return is higher.

With these criteria in mind, it is possible to consider other investment opportunities.

Note: All of these income ideas can be done in partnership with other organizations.

3. Financial Planning

How much money does your organization have in reserve? How much do the monthly operations cost? Can you afford to hire someone or buy new equipment?

The answers to all of these questions can be answered when an organization does financial planning. It is basically keeping track of your financials and coming up with a plan of how to spend, invest, and raise the money that is needed.

Typically an organization should have a few months of cash in reserve to help it with sustainability and protect it against the unexpected. The more reserves an organization has, the more it is able to do long-term strategic planning. It is only with strategic planning that an organization is able to rally its resources and scale.

Scaling a social organization has the interesting twist that it is extremely risk averse in failing, as that would result in its existing clients who need its services being abandoned. So an organization has to have an extremely high level of confidence that it will scale successfully in order to move forward.

Financial planning is the linchpin for strategic planning and therefore the ability for an organization to scale.

Scaling has caused a problem in the social sector. As organizations are resistant to scaling and exposing their existing organization to risk, most nonprofits are extremely small and the social sector is fragmented. Each region or municipality has a small nonprofit serving a specific demand of the community. For instance, there might be a food bank in one township and ten minutes away there might be another food bank that is operated independently. These food banks might not work together and might not learn from each other.

We've seen in the for-profit sector that scaling can be beneficial. Scaling or growth can lead to benefits such as consolidated purchasing and cost savings, continuous improvement and collaboration, and better branding or the ability to meet the needs of larger clients. If a social organization were to learn from these best practices, it would also be able to provide a larger social impact.

Financial planning might be what is needed for the social sector to become more effective.

3.1 The financial plan

Financial plans are key to establishing the organization and ensuring that it is sustainable to ensure that expenses can be met for more than two years using multiple sources of revenue streams. You may find various sources for financial projections including your board, advisors, and committee members.

The financial plan includes the following:

- **Start-up expenses:** All costs of starting up the organization from the website to the equipment to the computer.

- **Sources of funding:** How are the start-up expenses and the first few months of expenses going to be paid for prior to the business becoming self-sustaining or profitable? The sourcing options for a social organization are covered in the next section.

- **Sales projections:** How many sales will the organization make? This should be by month or summed up by quarter. Usually it is beneficial to break this down by product or service and show both the total number and dollar value of these sales.

- **Income statement projections:** This should be by month for the first two years and show the amount of total profit that will be made, which is the total revenue minus the total expenses.

- **Cash flow projections:** This is by month for two years indicating how much money is projected to be in the bank at any given time. This is different from the income statement as it is based on physical payments and cash transferred, which can often take longer than when the sale actually happens.

- **Balance sheet statements:** This shows a one-day snapshot of the value of the organization based on what it has versus what it owes. This should be done quarterly in year one and at year-end after that. (See sample on the download kit.)

- **Break-even:** How many sales need to be made before the organization begins to make a profit? This should include the total start-up costs and the monthly expenses that are being incurred. Many social organizations don't expect to break even for up to five years, so this has significant impacts on the need for multiple sources of funding.

A key part of any financial plan is to outline and be fully aware of the assumptions that have been made. Often these are educated guesses, and this needs to be highlighted so that you can better evaluate your risk when making decisions based on this financial plan.

The financial plan is a segment of a business plan which can initially take the form of a lean canvas or one-page business plan which will be discussed in the next chapter. Plans are living documents and need to be changed as market conditions, new programming, and new ideas impact it.

4. Financial Sourcing

If a social organization that is first launching doesn't expect to be financially sustainable for five to eight years, there is a heavy reliance on sourcing additional financing. This is critical to getting the idea off the ground.

Once an organization is financially sustainable, there are often additional financial sourcing sought for new endeavors or ongoing research and development. Financial sourcing is always an important part of the social organization.

4.1 Grants

It is interesting to note that grants are a continuum of funding sources that are available within the social sector. In fact, they are increasingly used in the initial stage to help the ideas be seeded and get off the ground, whereas loans and some of the other tools are helping to scale the ideas.

The challenges with grants is that they are often limited and have a significant amount of regulations around them including the reporting requirements. As granting programs have changed over the last few decades, there are fewer that provide core funding to organizations and it is almost impossible to become one of the organizations that receive them if you don't already have one. In addition, there are fewer grants that provide infrastructure and admin support, with more being focused on the programs themselves.

With these changes and restrictions, more and more organizations are considering other alternatives.

4.2 Loans

Not all organizations are able to sustain loans or they perceive loans as risky. However, loans often have fewer restrictions than grants and can be in larger amounts.

Traditional banks have historically stayed away from the social sector, concerned with being put in the awkward position of having to foreclose on a nonprofit or social enterprise. There are some that will do this work, but can be at higher interest rates as these organizations are perceived as more risky when working with traditional lenders.

Nontraditional lenders are now entering the space including community foundations, family foundations, and corporate foundations. These investors are often more lenient with the social organizations in terms of interest rates and payment terms, offering preferable rates. As these investors have a social lens to this work, they might structure a portion of the loan to be forgivable or even grant a portion to help in the growth of the organization.

4.3 Philanthropic angel investors/venture capitalists

Angel investors and venture capitalists have also entered the space. They have a philanthropic lens as many successful business people attribute their success to the communities that they came from, and so they often wish to donate back to society.

These investors are willing to be flexible with either loans or equity as they are not a foundation which would have limitations on the structures that they are able to support. This allows for a lot of creativity. Often it isn't just their financial resources, but also their networks and business acumen that can be supportive for these social organizations.

The great news is that there is a growing number of these individuals! However, the infrastructure and networks to find these investors and them to find you has not yet matured. More regions are working on developing these networks. But as for any business, the best thing to do is to start talking about what your organization does and who you are looking for. The more people you tell, the more likely you will be connected to them.

4.4 Community bond

Community bond is a tool where community members provide funds on a low-rate basis repayable in the future when income is earned. This is most successful for infrastructure projects such as purchasing a wind turbine or purchasing real estate. It is important to have it set up so that there is a return and also that the community bond is secured through the asset that is being purchased.

There are a few examples in North America where this model has already been used. Increasingly, organizations are looking at this model and experimenting with its use. The legislation is still in its infancy, but there is a general willingness to support this social finance tool.

4.5 Crowdfunding online

Crowdfunding online is a method to attract individuals or groups who may want to preorder products or just be involved in a venture. The methodology is similar to fundraising, and there are sites that help with the transaction and getting awareness about the campaign. The site takes a percentage of the funding that is raised.

Theater Company on Kickstarter

A theater company is looking to launch a new show. They decide to use crowdfunding to get it off the ground and purchase the costumes and supplies needed for the performance. By going on the site they can presell tickets to the show or have the star actor sign a poster to entice people to crowdfund the new show.

This is starting to develop from simply a way to preorder or make a donation to giving the public an option to invest in the organization as equity or loan.

Thankfully, the supports of finance for the social sector are getting stronger. In fact, many social investors will remark that the returns and the margins of investing in social organization exclusively is higher than the traditional for-profit investment. As more investors are interested in this space, there is a risk that the number of profitable investments will decrease. But there is the other thought that as the social finance sector continues to grow, there will be more social organizations encouraged to get started.

5. Monitoring

Finally, when finance and numbers are involved, the organization needs to monitor and report back to the stakeholders involved.

5.1 Record keeping

A paper-based record-keeping system should be established to support online systems. This could be a numeric system, an alpha system, or an alphanumeric system and should have similarities to the computer record system.

Some records will need to be maintained for taxation purposes for several years (six or more) as the governing department can perform audits to ensure accurate filing of data and supporting documents.

For other records you should include an expiry date for archiving purposes.

5.2 Banking reports

Monthly reporting (including bank statement reconciliation) must be produced to management and the board of directors as a package of financial reports including variances to the plan.

5.3 Investor reports

Investor reports may also be needed and may include grant funding organizations and government progress status reports. Each of them might have different specifications of information that they need.

Some things to consider:

- **Outputs:** What are the quantifiable benefits that have happened due to the funding that was received? Were more people employed? Sheltered? Benefited in some way?

- **Outcomes:** What are the stories and qualitative benefits that you have captured along the way (i.e., clearly identify the impacts on the parties involved in the program).

- **Key learnings:** Something will always go wrong. The funders want to know that you learned from this and adapted. Including this in the report will help their confidence in funding you in the future or in helping them work with other organizations like yours.

5.4 Stakeholder reports

It is always a good idea to overcommunicate. Are there other people who are impacted by the organization that should have a report as well? Many social organizations produce an annual report or monthly newsletter to update everyone in the community. By doing this, the social organization remains top of mind.

This can also take the form of published articles for journals and magazines, or presentations to a variety of audiences as part of informing and messaging.

CHAPTER 8
ACTIONS SPEAK LOUDER
THAN WORDS

At some point the rubber needs to hit the road. You are at the point of action when you are ready to go beyond the planning and start doing things. These things include registering the business, getting business cards, and setting up a website. This is when we move from what we should do, to what we are doing.

Action and execution is the next step. For the sustainability of your organization, the ability to implement the action plan is the deciding factor of success.

Often people find this transition difficult to make. Why? There are some critical skill sets that people have who more easily go from planning to execution:

- **Task oriented:** Most people are either naturally more strategic thinkers or linear thinkers. Often, to come up with a great idea and to be able to come up with the strategic plan behind the idea, requires nonlinear thinking and more strategic thinkers. However, when focused on action, the requirement changes and favors the linear thinker who can move through the tasks quickly without being distracted. So it requires a change in thinking to get the implementation started!

- **Self-motivated:** Getting started on the actions takes some self-motivation. Staying on task and keeping oneself motivated is more difficult and more important. Having tactics to do this or naturally being self-motivated helps in moving the action plan forward.

- **Risk taking:** People are naturally risk averse. Even perceived risk takers are actively seeking to reduce their risk. Getting the action plan started is an emotional time. All of the assumptions and the core ideals of the plan will be put to the test and often there will be a need to pivot, if not make a U-turn. Putting an idea out there is a hard thing to do and even veterans will admit that it doesn't get any easier.

It is barely possible to get the work done that needs to be done, and still get your sleep. That requires superior organizational skills. Which leads us to the fourth skill set:

- **Organization:** Being organized can help with the other important skill sets. By having a plan in place you can help become task oriented, you keep motivated especially as you are tracking your process, and it appears less risky when you can track your process and record when you need to pivot. It also takes discipline to schedule time for tasks to be done that are prioritized.

The organization behind the action is what this chapter is all about: How to create your action plan and be organized enough to actually do it.

1. Introduction to Action Plans

Action plans are the methodology that ties your organizational strategy to the tactics that need to be accomplished to reach these strategic goals. They set you up for tracking purposes and they provide a vision for where you are headed.

It is the plan that pushes down the strategy to design the tactics. Then it is the results of the tactics that push back feedback of what the future strategy should be.

2. The Strategic Plan

Strategic planning is figuring out the logical way to achieve your goals. The strategy is always tied to how your organization is different than the others in a way that matters to its stakeholders.

In for-profit, a common way to be different is to have a higher quality product than the competition, or at a lower price. For example, if a hotel is four stars and has a competitive price, that is its strategy against the competition for a specific type of customer. There could be other hotels in the area that are five stars and higher pricing, whereas there could be three-star hotels at lower prices. But there is a type of customer that will prefer what the four star hotel is offering at the price. This blend of quality and price allows them to maximize their profit.

In nonprofit or social enterprise, there are more variables that need to be factored in. It isn't always about selling products and services. They don't just have one customer. And the social impact is more important than profit alone.

2.1 The vision

The vision is a statement that is clear about where your organization is headed. The best visions do the following:

- **Give clear direction:** The vision should be clear about the direction that the organization is going. This is where you want to be in the next five to ten years. It is the guiding light of the organization. Having a metric could be helpful to remove any vagueness.

- **Offer inspiration:** A vision should be motivating for the volunteers, employees, and the stakeholders. Some visions stretch the organization so much that it might never be reached, but it is continuously inspiring.

- **Are helpful when making decisions**: A vision should be helpful in making strategic decisions. Every time there is a fork in the road, it is helpful to have the vision that determines which path to take.

To get started in creating your vision you need to think about who you are helping and in what you wish to help them.

2.1a Who are you impacting?

As opposed to for-profit visions which are very company focused, the nonprofit or social enterprise vision is focused on the clients and stakeholders that are impacted by the organization.

The scope of who is being considered needs to be part of the vision. The scope could be very small or exceptionally broad. The common targets of people being impacted include:

- **Clients**: The primary client is the main marginalized community or individual in need helped through the nonprofit or social enterprise.

- **Clients and volunteers**: The scope expands by being concerned with both the end client as well as the volunteers that are part of the solution. This is the understanding that everyone involved benefits and needs support from each other.

- **Clients, volunteers, employees, donors, and funders**: The organization may wish to positively impact everyone it touches and is involved in the organization. This scope recognizes that every action has a reaction, and everyone needs to be considered.

- **Community**: The community focus is when the organization has expanded the scope and recognized a larger focus on creating systematic change (or change that lasts) in society. This could be local, regional/county, state/province, national, or global.

2.1b How much are you helping them?

Once an organization has the scope of the target that it is focused on, it has to decide how it will help them. Some organizations are focused on simply helping the end clients with their immediate needs, whereas others wish to make a deeper impact. The continuum of social justice is as follows:

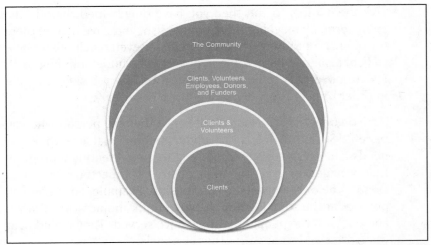

Figure 1: Who Are You Impacting?

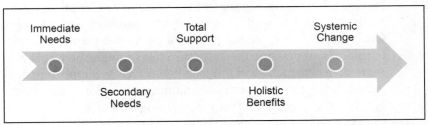

Figure 2: Continuum of Social Justice

- **Immediate needs:** What is the immediate concern? This is usually when referring to the clients and the most obvious challenge that they face. Example: For people in poverty, the most immediate need might be access to food.

- **Secondary needs:** There often isn't a single thing that the clients need. There is usually a plethora of things that would collectively make a bigger impact. Example: For people in poverty the secondary needs might include a place to sleep, haircuts, dental health, and other basic services that would improve their lives.

- **Total support:** This is the understanding that meeting immediate and secondary needs won't change the person's life in the long term. What type of programming could make a long-term impact? Often the old saying used is that you'd rather teach people how to fish than provide them with the fish to eat. If you give them a fish to eat, then you have only helped them in the short term. By teaching them how to fish, you have helped them for the rest of their lives. And they might even teach others how to fish! Example: For people in poverty, the understanding to alleviate poverty is to help with education and job skills training in order to help the individual get out of poverty.

- **Holistic benefits:** The end client is not the only person who can benefit. Social justice is the understanding that everyone has needs and everyone has something to give. Creating a program that provides for everyone to be positively impacted rather than there to be only a give/take relationship. Example: For people in poverty, at the soup kitchen the volunteers should also sit down and eat with the people that they have served. They would hear the stories and treat each other as equals.

- **Systemic change:** The final part of the continuum is focused on making a long-term benefit to the existing clients but for future people in need as well. It is to create a program and advocacy work that makes it so that the need no longer exists. Example: For people in poverty, the systemic change might be to provide more access to skills and job training as well as supporting economic development in the communities or regions where poverty is more prevalent. This type of programming would create the foundations to eradicate poverty from the area.

Often organizations begin by recognizing the immediate needs, but as they mature as organizations they recognize and are able to support more of the continuum.

2.1c Creating the vision

Now the vision has to come together. It needs to be phrased in a way that gives clear direction, is inspiring, and is helpful in decision making. It needs to be clear on the scope of who will be impacted and it needs to be clear on how it will help them.

Examples:

- No family will go hungry.

- Everyone who wants a job is given the chance.

- We will cure cancer in our lifetime.

- Everyone's childhood dream can come true.

All of the above can include a measurable target and initial location(s).

2.2 The mission

How do you live out the vision each day? The mission guides the steps of the employees and the volunteers throughout their day-to-day tasks. It is also a litmus test of whether the right tasks each day are being done.

The mission is more specific in how the vision will be accomplished and describes the purpose of the organization. This should be tied to the vision as something that is more tangible. Here are some examples in Table 2.

Table 2
Vision to Mission

Vision	Mission
No family will go hungry.	We feed people in need each day.
Everyone who wants a job is given a chance.	We "re-skill" people to be employment ready.
We will cure cancer in our lifetime.	We deliver leading-edge cancer research.
Everyone's childhood dream can come true.	We support collaborative communities.

2.3 The future of strategy

Strategic planning is a concept whereby the leaders of an organization meet on a prescribed schedule to do the strategic planning collective. There might be a facilitator and there is a defined amount of time that is dedicated to this process.

Recently there has been a change in how this is done as strategic planning and its processes are too linear. Instead, strategic thinking has emerged with the understanding that defined timelines only once or twice a year limit the amount of nonlinear thinking that is required for the development of a great strategy.

Strategic thinking is the understanding that things continuously evolve and adapt to the changing environment, and a fluid strategy is more responsive. If there are various understandings of scope and ways to support the target clients, then this could change outside of the prescribed times and the organization could adapt on the fly.

For example, strategic thinking would allow a food bank to be more flexible. If a hairstylist offered to come by once a month, a strategic-thinking food bank would be adaptive enough to accept the kind offer. Then it would potentially experiment further with other services. In this way, the food bank has expanded its understanding of the impact it can make without needing a strategic planning session.

3. The Action Plan

With the strategy in place, the social organization now has to develop a plan to make this happen. These are the tasks that have to happen to allow the organization to get closer to achieving its vision.

To move forward, it is important to understand where you are today. You can't figure out where to go if you don't know where you are now. You can do this by figuring out what your organization's strengths, weaknesses, opportunities, and threats are. (See Sample 14.)

- What are the strengths of your organization including the benefits?
    - How many of your target group are you already supporting?
    - How much are you impacting them?
- What are the weaknesses of your organization now?
- What are the external opportunities that your organization could leverage?
- What are the external threats that your organization needs to mitigate?

This should all be listed for help in planning your next steps.

3.1 Implementation plan

Based on how your organization is situated today, the next priority is to come up with the tactics that will get you where you want to be.

Make a list of action items. For each part of the understanding of where you are today, you need to brainstorm strategically about how to optimize or minimize these:

Sample 14
Soup Kitchen SWOT

Strengths (Internal and Positive):	Weaknesses (Internal and Negative):
- Feeding more 100 people a day - Full time and dedicated volunteers - Good full-time chef - Good space for serving	- Few part-time volunteers - High turnover in staff (non-chef) - Old equipment in the kitchen
Opportunities (External and Positive):	**Threats (External and Negative):**
- Good relationships with local farmers - Good for the summer and fall - Good recognition in the city	- No relationships with the grocery stores or restaurants - No wintertime supplies - Funding from the foundation is decreasing

- Are there ways to improve the strengths or opportunities that you already have?

- Are there ways to minimize or reduce the weaknesses or threats?

- Are there ways that the strengths could synergize with the external opportunities and be to your advantage?

- Are there ways that the strengths or opportunities could minimize or eliminate the current weaknesses or threats?

- Is there any way to leverage the strengths and opportunities to help move towards the vision?

Example: Soup Kitchen

- Could the soup kitchen leverage its good recognition in the city to do a volunteer drive?

- Could the good recognition help with a fundraising initiative to offset the funding lost by the foundation?

- Could relationships in the community allow it to expand beyond serving food?

- Could the chef expand the programming beyond food?

- Could some of the 100 people served help as employees/volunteers?

Each of these actions would then be prioritized based on matching the mission and in moving towards the vision. This prioritized order can then be turned into a schedule of actions.

4. Measuring Results

Being able to measure the social impact of a social organization's work is critical to being able to see if it is doing its work successfully. In the for-profit world, it is easy to measure as everything is based on financials, which are quantifiable and relatively objective.

In the nonprofit and social enterprise space, where financials are secondary to social impact when it comes to measuring success, being able to measure the social impact takes priority. Not only is it crucial to being able to determine if something it working, but it is also important to help identify how to improve. The ability to measure an organization's social impact also allows it to communicate to its staff, volunteers, donors, and other stakeholders in a quantifiable way.

When should a social organization start thinking about measurement? From the beginning. Typically an organization just starts to try to make an impact, and measurement is secondary. But from the very beginning an organization needs to figure out how to qualify and quantify its results. See the download kit for a logframe (logical framework), which is a way to look at a project's goal, anticipated work, and eventual results.

The main things to measure are:

- **Inputs:** What is put into the organization to make the social impact?

- **Outputs:** What are the quantifiable ways that the organization is making a difference?

- **Outcomes:** What are the qualifiable ways that the organization is making a difference (i.e., what impacts it is having)?

- **Impacts:** What are the long-term impacts that have been made?

Note: Social Return on Investment (SROI) is a common way for a project or organization to measure its impact. However, as social impact measurement becomes more advanced, there is an understanding that SROI is relatively subjective and there is no standard format for it. Each organization might measure differently what is considered an investment, and each organization might measure the social return differently. This inconsistency is making SROI less standard.

4.1 Inputs

Inputs are all of the investments that the social organization is putting in to get results. Measuring the inputs is important, as you need to be able to understand how much has been spent or invested into the outcomes.

This can include:

- **Financial inputs:** Was equipment purchased or what are all of the start-up costs? All of the financial inputs of the organization into the project or program needs to be included.

- **Volunteer inputs:** Time is money. This also counts for volunteers. If they weren't spending their time on one project, program, or organization, this time could be spent somewhere else. There is value here, and that needs to be added up.

- **Employee inputs:** How much time employees including the management have spent on the program or project. This can be quantified based on the hourly wages of the employees or the entire salary.

- **Partnership inputs:** For partners of the social organization to work and invest their resources into a project or program, they are not able to spend their resources elsewhere.

All of these inputs can be quantified and added up to understand the total investment of the organization or a specific project or program.

4.2 Outputs

Outputs are the quantifiable results that the program or project has created. Often it is difficult to ensure that what is being measured is directly caused by the project itself, and there is an entire science behind this measurement. Outputs are helpful as they are a specific number and something that can be compared and understood. However, it is not always the whole story.

Some common types of outputs to measure include:

- The number of clients supported by the programs.

- The specific result that the clients have such as a new job, ability to graduate high school, or other future outputs.

4.3 Outcomes

Outcomes are like outputs, but they are qualitative. These are the stories and other subjective change that have occurred due the program or project. Some types of outcomes include:

- The most unexpected thing that occurred due to the program.
- The stories of the clients who were impacted.
- The stories of the volunteers, staff, or other stakeholders who were impacted through the product or program.
- Secondary impacts that were not quantified (as they were unexpected).
- Predicted cause and effect changes that happened that are not directly attributable to the program or project.

Increasingly the outcomes of the projects or programs are considered equally important as to the outputs that are measured, sometimes even more so. Gathering this information can be done through surveys with clients, family, volunteers, and even staff. These results are usually needed to support grant reporting and to government and corporations who provide support.

4.4 Impact

The final impact is the long-term impact that has occurred. This is often a systemic change or a more widely important impact. Some examples of this:

- More economic development in a region based on employment rates, literacy rates, average GDP, or another metric of national importance.
- The way that the entire industry works in some important way such as the adoption of technology or collaboration.
- The growth or success of a subsector as a whole due in part of the project or initiative.
- The change in attitude about an issue.

- Advocacy and policy change on a specific issue.

These are long-term impacts that have dramatically changed a subsector.

5. Bringing It Together

Putting all of these pieces into one place helps to communicate to everyone the intentions of the social organization. The employees and volunteers can use this information to help guide their actions, but it also helps to motivate them and allows these engaged individuals to talk positively about the plans for the organization.

The funders and donors can gain confidence when they see the thought process of the organization and the plan for making an even bigger difference. A lot of these best practices come from thinking about social justice, volunteer retention, the various stakeholders and communications, and it all comes together to lend more credibility to why these funders and donors should continue to contribute to the cause.

Depending on what needs to be communicated and how this needs to be communicated, there are a few different templates that could be used:

- **A one-page business plan:** A one-page business plan is brief, however, it has the same categories as a longer business plan would have, and is summarized for the same reasons as a lean canvas (more on that below). Often it is more difficult for someone to write less than more. This is perfect for someone who needs to write a business plan but the audience is either a small team or less formal communication is needed. (See sample on the download kit for a one-page business plan).

- **Lean canvas:** The lean canvas is a single page of information that summarizes the strategy and action plans of the organization. This is lean as it doesn't have unnecessary information and is easy for the reader to review. It is also called a canvas because it is something that is visual for people to be able to put up on a wall and add to. This is often used during the ideation and start-up stage of a business to test whether the idea is a good one. It saves time and allows for flexibility in the early stages while being an effective communication tool. (See sample on the download kit).

- **Detailed business plan:** A business plan includes all of the details regarding the strategy and tactics of the organization. This is often written in order to get financing from a bank or from other investors that want to see more detailed information. The business plan would be accompanied with detailed financial projections. This is often necessary for a business loan or for a larger audience.

In any social enterprise or nonprofit, the most important thing is going to be passion and the ability to implement. With any idea it is always 1 percent inspiration and 99 percent perspiration.

CONCLUSION:
THE FUTURE OF SOCIAL ENTERPRISE AND SOCIAL INNOVATION

The world is changing, for the better. But there is more change to come!

Society is thinking more holistically, but this continues to take on new frontiers. Gender equality, racism, food poverty, and global warming are common topics around the water cooler. These are conversations that were not happening before. With discussion, with understanding, and with compassion, even more change for the better is possible.

The language of social enterprise has emerged. B Corps are gaining traction and brand awareness. New ideas are hitting the mainstream. Other language is emerging such as "social procurement" and "social investment." More functional areas of existing businesses are starting to reflect on how they can make a difference within the realms of control that they have.

Corporate Social Responsibility is now a mandatory part of being in business. Plus it is trickling into all sizes of business from very large multinationals to the independent businesses. There is an understanding that this is part of the responsibility of being in business and contributing back to society.

Business best practices are being embraced. Nonprofits and social enterprises alike understand that it isn't enough to just have a good cause. If for-profit businesses are starting to make CSR a mandatory part of doing business, then social initiatives have to start being competitive when it comes to their offerings. That means that business practices are no longer taboo, they are a mandatory part of doing a social initiative well. They need to be leveraged at the risk of falling behind and not being able to fulfill the mission. Online marketing continues to evolve. With all of the changes in online media, marketing is changing for everyone. Social initiatives need to be staying up to speed on this.

Volunteer management is becoming an art. Being innovative is important to engage new volunteers and retain the great ones.

Operational efficiencies are coming. With both partnerships and technologies in the pipeline, nonprofits and social enterprises can realize economies of scale and other efficiencies. Supply chains are under scrutiny and have created a new opening for social initiatives. The 100-Mile Diet, fair trade, recycling programs, and serving developing countries have created new opportunities and new supply chains recently.

Finances have changed, but new models are being tested. One example is Purpose Capital, an organization that specializes in social finance that works with nonprofits and social enterprises throughout North America. It creates new social finance tools that are best suited to new and unique situations. Crowdfunding and community bonds are just the beginning of a new wave of social investment options.

Implementation is critical, but so is impact measurement. More often than not the outcomes of a social initiative are different than originally intended. Communities in Africa that were given mosquito nets to sleep in used them as fishing nets. It didn't make less of an impact, but it was an unintended and important to measure impact.

So what does the future hold? The following are some trends we hope to keep seeing.

1. A Focus on Growth

Why help one geographical region and client when a social initiative could make a large impact across a country or region and for multiple clients? Social franchising is a trend with models popping up internationally. Large nonprofits with legacy infrastructure are researching how to repurpose these assets and pivot to become relevant and impactful. Social franchising might be a way forward.

2. Collaboration and Partnerships

Collaboration and partnerships have always been important. But with the emphasis on them when it comes to grant applications and the results that many social initiatives have seen due to partnering, it is more than lip service. Partnerships can be with share platforms where multiple social initiatives use the same governance structure, boards of directors, and administration. Partnerships can be through joint ventures where entirely new structures are created.

3. Top of Mind Awareness in the Media and Society As a Whole

Social justice, societal issues, and the social initiatives that are trying to do something about it are all being given a large amount of press. The media gathers these stories as they are of interest to their audiences, but often these stories also change or impact the perceptions of the readers. This type of media is called "generative journalism," when the story is to influence or change the reader's viewpoint.

What is the hope here? When there are a lot of stories about social initiatives, more people will think that doing socially responsible things is better accepted by society, which will in turn result in more social initiatives and stories. It is an upward spiral!

With these trends and what is already happening, there is no doubt that the world is changing for the better and your social initiative can help it on its way.

DOWNLOAD KIT

Please enter the URL you see in the box below into a web browser on your computer to access and use the download kit.

> **www.self-counsel.com/updates/giveback/17kit.htm**

The following is included in the download kit:

- Samples, resources, and forms for you to use in your social enterprise

service@self-counsel.com